SOCIAL SERVICES: WORKING UNDER PRESSURE

Edited by Susan Balloch, John McLean and Mike Fisher

with Toby Andrew, Dorothy Buglass, Barbara Davey, Linda Dolan, Jay Ginn, Winifred McConkey and Jan Pahl

The POLICY

PRESS

First published in Great Britain in 1999 by

The Policy Press
University of Bristol
34 Tyndalls Park Road
Bristol BS8 1PY
UK

Tel   +44 (0)117 973 8797
Fax   +44 (0) 117 973 7308
e-mail   tpp@bristol.ac.uk
http://www.bristol.ac.uk/Publications/TPP

The National Institute for Social Work receives support from the Department of Health. The research reported here was funded by the Department of Health, the Department of Health and Social Services (the Northern Ireland Office) and the Central Research Unit (the Scottish Office). The views expressed are those of the authors and not necessarily those of funding bodies.

British Library Cataloguing in Publication Data
A catalogue record for this book is available from the British Library

ISBN 1 86134 137 7

Cover design: Qube Design Associates, Bristol.

Printed and bound in Great Britain by Hobbs the Printers Ltd, Southampton.

Contents

Acknowledgements

Several people who played an important part in shaping the Workforce studies reported in this book were not able to contribute to this latest account. We wish to place on record our thanks to Hazel Qureshi, Dhanwant Rai and Jenny Williams, who were originally members of the Workforce research team. Over the years, we have also benefited from the advice of Fabian Best and Colin Taylor, and we thank them and other members of the Advisory Group for their contribution.

The research was funded by the Department of Health in England, the Department of Health and Social Services in Northern Ireland, and by the Central Research Unit in the Scottish Office. We thank these agencies for their support and for the liaison work undertaken respectively by Dr Ruth Chadwick, Eleanor Simpson and Fiona Fraser.

Grateful thanks are also due to Veronica Barker, whose patience and secretarial skills greatly added to the consistency and presentation of the text, to Rose Freeman, our Administrator, and to the Library and Information staff at the National Institute for Social Work (NISW) for their support.

Finally, our study would not have been possible without the support of the five local authorities in England, the four Health and Social Services Boards (as then) in Northern Ireland, and the two social work districts (as then) in Scotland. The work reported here depended entirely on the willingness of a wide variety of staff to arrange access and to be interviewed. We hope that we have done justice to the wealth of information they provided.

Notes on contributors

Susan Balloch is Director of Policy at the National Institute for Social Work (NISW). As Senior Researcher in NISW's Research Unit she was responsible for the management of the Workforce studies. She has lectured in social policy at Goldsmiths College and worked to develop anti-poverty strategies at the Association of Metropolitan Authorities. Publications include studies of the effects of unemployment on social services, anti-poverty strategy, credit unions, refugees, local government charging policies and the social services workforce.

John McLean is a Researcher at the National Institute for Social Work. He has previously worked in residential and field social work with older people, children and adolescents, users with severe learning difficulties and users with mental health problems, including work as an Approved Social Worker. Publications include studies of responses to health education on HIV, and the work experience of social services staff in relation to gender, job stress, commitment, violence and anti-discriminatory practice and sexuality.

Mike Fisher joined the Research Unit in July 1996 as Director. He was previously Senior Lecturer in the School for Policy Studies, University of Bristol and is a qualified Social Worker. His research interests include community care, practice knowledge in social work and social care, gender and caring, user studies and user-led research, and computer-assisted qualitative data analysis. He is currently working on studies of commitment and inclusiveness in the social services workforce programme.

Toby Andrew previously worked at the Addiction Research Unit at the Institute of Psychiatry and is a member of the Royal Statistical Society. His interests include the development of outcome measures, statistical analysis and the implementation of research methodology, developing the measurement of commitment in the social services workforce and the analysis of outcome measures for older people with dementia. He is currently working at St Thomas's Hospital as a Genetic Epidemiologist.

Dorothy Buglass was born in North Shields, Northumberland, and educated at London University. She has lived in Edinburgh for many years where she has carried out research in social psychiatry and social work. She has worked in medical, local authority and voluntary organisation settings and is now an independent researcher.

Barbara Davey joined the Research Unit in December 1995 from the Centre for Institutional Studies at the University of East London. She is currently working on analysis of women and career progression in the social services as well as the Social and Health Care Study. Her research interests include gender and work issues, the social and health care interface, statistical analysis and research methodology.

Linda Dolan is currently employed as a researcher at Royal Holloway, University of London, where she is involved in research evaluating the respite care needs of children with disabilities. Her research interests include education and workforce-related issues and health and social services provision. She was employed as a Research Assistant at the National Institute for Social Work from 1995 to 1997.

Jay Ginn is currently employed in the Sociology Department at Surrey University, researching the changing pensions mix in Britain. She has published widely on women's employment and pensions. Books (co-authored/co-edited with Sara Arber) include *Gender and later life* (1991) and *Connecting gender and ageing* (1995). She was employed as a Researcher at the National Institute for Social Work from 1994 to 1996.

Winifred McConkey has spent her working life in social work practice and in social work training in Northern Ireland. She has worked part-time as a Researcher in Northern Ireland for NISW since 1994.

Jan Pahl is Professor of Social Policy at the University of Kent at Canterbury. Her previous job was as Director of Research at the National Institute for Social Work, where she was responsible for initiating the research on the social services workforce which is the topic of this book. She also has a long-standing interest in the control and allocation of money within the household and is currently engaged in a study of new forms of money and family financial arrangements.

List of tables and figures

Technical note on tables

Throughout the book, the percentages in tables are generally calculated with a sample weighting applied. To avoid the complexity of showing unweighted sample sizes and *Base* numbers in each table, unweighted sample sizes are generally given only in the main tables in each chapter, and are not duplicated in the rest of the chapter. There are some exceptions to this. For example in Chapter Six, *Base* numbers are included in the tables on experience of racism and discrimination. *Base* numbers are given in these tables because of the over-sampling of black staff and because the calculations concern one data set only, the English study. All data in the book have been presented in greater detail in previous reports and the tables in the book represent a summary of the main findings. Where percentages for the three studies appear in tables, these have generally been calculated separately, and are shown for comparative purposes: unless otherwise stated therefore, tests of significance do not refer to differences between the samples. Tests of significance are indicated as *p<0.05, **p<0.01 and ***p<0.001.

Tables

Figures

ONE

Introduction

Susan Balloch, Dorothy Buglass and Winifred McConkey

Throughout the United Kingdom major changes have been taking place in social care, giving new and complex responsibilities to the estimated third of a million social services staff. The separation of purchasing and providing, and the move to the mixed economy of welfare, have placed the social services on the divide between the public and private sectors. The distinction between health care and social care has become increasingly blurred as expanding residential and domiciliary services have sought to meet the needs of the growing population of frail older people in a period of financial stringency. Consumerism has emphasised users' and carers' rights and needs and the importance of social services staff being responsive to these. At the same time, scandals given prominence in the media, particularly in child protection and residential care, have focused attention on the training and regulation of social care staff and stimulated the demand for performance indicators, measures of quality and guidelines for good practice.

It is surprising that, against this background, there has been little research into the people whose working lives have been most affected by these developments, even though this workforce provides an exceptional window through which to look at the social services as a whole and to assess the impact of recent change. There is monitoring work, such as that undertaken by the Local Government Management Board and the Association of Directors of Social Service to examine flows into and out of the social services workforce (LGMB, 1997a), and that undertaken by the Central Council for Education and Training in Social Work (CCETSW) to explore the success of qualified social workers in gaining employment (CCETSW, 1996). In these studies, analysis is very much focused on the immediate questions of supply and demand, rather than on the history or experience of the workforce. Only recently was work begun on a comprehensive human resources strategy which recognised the need for more active management of the social services' most valuable asset (LGMB/CCETSW, 1997). What has been missing has been an in-depth account of the origins and dynamics of social services staff.

The Workforce studies, on which this book is based, have addressed this by looking at both the work histories and current work experience of over 2,000 staff in the statutory social services in England, Scotland and Northern Ireland. (The Welsh Office felt it was not feasible for Wales to be included in the study because of the demands made on local authorities by the major reorganisation of local government then taking place.) Our research was initiated in 1992 with three broad aims (Qureshi and Pahl, 1992). The first was to develop an understanding of the structure and dynamics of the statutory social services workforce, looking at who worked in the social services, differences in career patterns between women and men, and different ethnic groups, their ambitions and their propensity to leave or stay in social services work. The second aim was to investigate the experience of working in social services in terms of job satisfaction and stress. Here we hoped to identify those aspects of work which staff found most rewarding, or which caused greatest dissatisfaction, and to provide more detailed evidence on problems such as violence, racism and discrimination which were beginning to emerge as serious issues. The third aim was to assess developments in training and to investigate the access to training of different groups of staff. We were interested in finding out what qualifications people had obtained before they joined the workforce, what training they had received in the course of their employment and what they hoped to undertake in the future. In particular, we were concerned about their responses to the new forms of training, such as National Vocational Qualifications (NVQs) and Scottish Vocational Qualifications (SVQs), and post-qualifying training.

Using this book

Drawing on the extensive survey material, this book explores the work histories of social services staff, describes their current jobs and examines their work experiences. Having read this first chapter, which explains both the background to the survey and the main instruments and concepts employed, readers may find it useful to read Chapter Three on the changing nature of work, but thereafter should feel free to move straight to the issue or issues of most interest. The book provides detailed evidence of abuse and violence at work, satisfaction and stress in the workplace, staff's experiences of racism and discrimination, gender issues and education and training. Further details of the chapters in which these are discussed are given at the end of this chapter. Though some chapters, such as Chapter Two, may present more statistical analysis than others, all findings are clearly explained in the text.

Our major research instrument was a longitudinal survey with a panel drawn from a sample of social services staff in five local authorities in England. A background to this is provided in the published research proposal which includes a review of the literature on which it was based, and a report on training in social services departments (Qureshi and Pahl, 1992; Rai, 1994). Subsequently, the survey was extended to two social work districts in Scotland and the four Boards and their Trusts in Northern Ireland. The English sample was first interviewed between October 1993 and February 1994 and the findings subsequently published in *Working in the social services* (Balloch et al, 1995). Further reports, again based on the first interviews, include *Working in the social services: A comparison of five local authorities in England* (Balloch et al, 1996) and *Work histories of social services staff* (Ginn et al, 1997). The second interviews took place between October and December 1995. Reports of these have so far been published for Northern Ireland (McConkey et al, 1997) and Scotland (Buglass et al, 1998).

For pragmatic purposes our study was confined to the four broad job types of manager, field social work staff, home care worker and residential worker. Given the emphasis on managerialism as a force shaping social welfare in the 1990s (Kelly, 1991; Pollitt, 1993; Newman and Clarke, 1994), social services managers have remained curiously marginal to research on either social care or management, although knowledge of their background would have gone a long way to informing recent studies of community care implementation in which managers appeared to be distancing their practice from social work (Nixon, 1993; Lewis and Glennerster, 1996). Such findings would be challenged by Levin and Webb's study which showed a group of senior managers whose major job satisfaction lay in 'making a difference', that is, helping service users (Levin and Webb, 1997), suggesting their motivations may closely resemble those of front-line professional staff (see Chapter Four on sources of job satisfaction). Levin and Webb's work also points to a group of managers concerned about the pace of change, about maintaining staff morale and about increasing demands for services, all of which encouraged us to explore their levels of stress and job satisfaction.

The working experience of field social work staff has been subject to rather more investigation. An early study by Knapp and colleagues examined turnover among social workers in relation to educational qualification, but the data originated from 1975 and related to a very different workforce, in which, for example, 59% of field social workers lacked a relevant professional qualification (Knapp et al, 1981). The work by Lyons and colleagues has used CCETSW employment survey data to explore longer-term patterns in social workers' careers, and raises issues about, for example, the gender composition of this category of the workforce given the declining numbers of male recruits (Lyons et al, 1995). The census-based study of qualified social workers and probation officers in the general population undertaken by the Office of National Statistics (ONS) gave an overview of the social work labour force under 55 (in 1993), and provided valuable data on the career longevity of social workers (74% were then working as social workers and had always done so since qualification) and on the motivations of staff not currently in service (Smyth, 1996). Finally, the 'Ready to practise?' studies in England and Scotland conducted by Marsh and Triseliotis examined a wide range of factors affecting the readiness to practise of newly qualified social workers up to nine months after qualifying. The findings questioned the effectiveness of much social work teaching and pointed to a surprising degree of similarity between the preparedness of social workers from widely differing backgrounds (Marsh and Triseliotis, 1996). The largest category of the social services workforce, home care staff, has been the least studied. The most recent general overview is from 1983 (Dexter and Harbert, 1983), and their work has rarely excited those writing about community care sufficiently to prompt study of home care staff as a workforce. McKeganey's work in Scotland focused on home care organisers, and portrayed them as a group highly motivated by the desire to help people, rather than by any wish to enact any specific policy (McKeganey, 1989). Detailed sociological study by Warren of home care staff portrayed women who placed work second to family in their life commitments, but who were nevertheless highly committed to the service users (Warren, 1990). Importantly, Warren showed how home care skills were rooted in women's everyday experience as wives and mothers, suggesting that qualification may be seen as unnecessary where skills are regarded as 'natural'. Both these studies suggest difficulties in engaging this section of the workforce in learning processes which underpin organisational change.

Studies of residential workers have focused mainly on the quality of care in children's homes (Sinclair and Gibbs, 1996), the low level of qualifications among staff (Lane, 1994; Hills et al, 1997; McLean and Andrew, 1998) and the level of violence (Brown et al, 1986; Norris with Kedward,

1990; Joseph Rowntree Foundation Findings, 1995). Most investigations have focused on the minority of staff who work with looked-after children (DoH, 1998) and have been related to various inquiries into child abuse (Hughes et al, 1986; Kahan and Levy, 1991; Utting, 1991; Skinner, 1992; Warner, 1992). However, the work experience of the majority of staff, care assistants in residential homes for older people, a workforce in many ways similar to home care workers, has not been the subject of the same level of investigation (Davis, 1989; Qureshi and Pahl, 1992).

There have, of course, been extensive studies of other workforces, and this material was drawn on to construct a number of the key areas in the interview schedule about job satisfaction, commitment, sickness absence, and the home–work interface (Qureshi and Pahl, 1992). Similarly, there have been extensive studies of such issues as management in the public sector, women and management, and ethnic diversity, although with notable exceptions the specific topic of social services or social care as an employment market has rarely been the focus. We have been driven to the conclusion, to which we will return in our final chapter, that the origins and dynamics of the very people who deliver welfare have been viewed as secondary issues.

In order to set the context for the studies, we will introduce each of the three study areas and illustrate some of the differences in structure and terminology that the survey had to encompass.

England

The present structure of the statutory social services is based on the Local Authorities Social Services Act (1970), implemented in 1971, which created large social services departments in each local authority in England and Wales on the recommendations of the Seebohm Report (1968). These departments combined the previous functions of local authority children's health and welfare departments. The probation service was not integrated with these and remains under Home Office jurisdiction. The statutory personal social services in England and Wales experienced rapid and unprecedented expansion until 1976 (Webb and Wistow, 1987) when financial retrenchment curtailed growth across most publicly funded bodies. In ensuing years, in spite of pressure put on services by high levels of unemployment (Balloch et al, 1985) restructuring, accompanied by a much slower rate of expansion, took place. Concern with decentralisation and deinstitutionalisation, which dominated policy making in the 1980s, was gradually superseded by the demands of more recent legislation. Thus the

1989 Children Act, the 1990 NHS and Community Care Act and, to a lesser extent the 1991 Criminal Justice Act demanded new approaches to the organisation of services and to staff recruitment and training. More recently the 1995 Carers' (Recognition and Services) Act and the 1996 Community Care (Direct Payments) Act has focused new attention on users' and carers' needs and rights. The White Paper published in November 1998 has since set out plans for eight commissions for care standards to regulate care services through regional inspectorates and a register of accredited staff that will have a major impact on the workforce (Secretary of State 1998, Cm 4169).

It is important to recognise the sheer numbers of people involved in the social services workforce. In September 1997, 229,000 whole time equivalents (WTEs) or 309,000 individuals were employed in the statutory social services in England, 58% of whom worked part-time (DoH, 1998). (The numbers of staff employed in a service may be measured in terms of their WTEs or in terms of the actual number of individuals concerned.) The figure of 229,000 represented a drop of about 4,500 in WTE staffing since September 1996. Of these staff, 50% were working in an area office, 29% in residential care, 14% in day care (not covered in our survey), 7% in strategic central management and 1% elsewhere.

Most staff are women, employed in residential or home care services and are unqualified, in contrast to the small core of qualified social workers responsible for field social work – 33,000 (WTEs) (DoH, 1998). The survey referred to earlier, of qualified social workers aged under 55 at the time of the 1991 Census, suggested there were 53,000 resident in England, of whom 80% were working in social services, 13% in other fields and 7% not at all. Nearly all of those working in social services, 78%, were working for statutory local authorities. Of the rest, 11% were working for the probation service and 8% for voluntary organisations (Smyth, 1996).

Although local authorities are still the main providers of services such as home care, day centres and meals on wheels, the increase of voluntary and private sector providers has been pronounced. By 1995, 29% of home help/care contact hours were being provided by the latter, compared with just 2% in 1992 (DoH 1996a). While the domiciliary market remains relatively underdeveloped, there has been striking growth in the provision of residential care. Following the impetus given by the 1984 Residential Homes Act the number of residents of homes for older people and younger physically disabled people increased by 26% to 244,113. Most of this increase was attributable to the private sector. Private homes more than doubled in number and voluntary homes increased by over a quarter while local authority homes decreased by a third (DoH, 1996a). Although statistics of the total workforce employed across all three sectors are not reliable, it has been estimated that well over a million staff work for the statutory, voluntary and private social services (LGMB/CCETSW 1997). With provision shifting to the voluntary and private sectors, the working conditions of these staff can be expected to change, with possible effects on service delivery and service users. Not only will actual employers change, but also terms and conditions of work, such as the extension of part-time working and the growth of agency work (Goodenough, 1996).

Such changes in employment patterns pose new problems for the recruitment and training of the workforce, making it imperative to search for new ways of maintaining standards, including the continuity of care, improving access to training and creating more effective regulation and inspection procedures. In some areas local government reorganisation has added to these changes, although the local authorities in which our research was carried out were not affected by this.

The English sample

The research took place in five local authorities, including one county council, two metropolitan boroughs, one inner London borough with a high level of deprivation and one more affluent outer London borough. These authorities are not intended to be representative of all English local authorities, though it is reasonable to think that each may serve as an example of its particular local authority type. Within each authority, however, the sample was fully representative of the four 'job types' we studied, that is, manager, field social work staff, home care worker and residential worker. Therefore, the findings of the survey reflect the structure and characteristics of the workforce, as we defined it, across these five authorities. The validity of the survey was subsequently supported by close similarities in the findings for each of the job types across the five authorities, and, in many cases, across the authorities in Scotland and Boards in Northern Ireland. Its findings also matched those of other national surveys very closely (LGMB, 1996).

Our research was limited to these four job types and excluded other groups such as day care staff and occupational therapists. Managers, defined as those with responsibilities for other staff, included strategic and area managers, team leaders, home care organisers and officers in charge of residential homes. Field social work staff included all those involved in field social work as well as social work assistants and a range of other support staff. Among the five authorities we found 90 different titles for jobs which were defined as manager and 70 different job titles for social work staff. The meanings of titles were not always clear. In some authorities, for example, a 'care manager' was a senior manager with responsibility for a substantial budget, whereas elsewhere this job title was used for front-line social workers with responsibility for the care of their own caseloads. The variety of titles reflected both local authority culture and the rapidly changing parameters of social services management and social work. It posed problems for drawing an accurate sample and for subsequent analysis. For the purposes of selecting the sample, staff were drawn randomly from computerised personnel lists, on the basis of records showing that staff worked in management, field social work, home care or residential work. The staff selected were categorised as far as possible into one of these four staff groups. Information was also collected on the staff's job title, work setting, responsibilities and grade, so that a more accurate job classification could be drawn up using the Department of Health's Social Services Staffing Return classification (SSDS001) and the more broadly used Standard Occupation Classification.

The original proposal for the English survey suggested that a sample of at least 1,000 staff should be maintained across the two interviews (Qureshi and Pahl, 1992). Because of the inaccuracy of local authority records, a large initial sample of 1,664 was drawn from the five authorities. Of these, 12% no longer worked for the relevant authority, and a further 13% refused or could not be contacted. Ultimately 1,276 were interviewed, an overall sample of 17% of the whole workforce in the five authorities (see Table 1.1, p 17 for details of the number of staff who took part in the first interview in each authority). Because drawing a simple random sample and would have produced a preponderance of home care and residential workers and would have led to an unacceptably small number of men and black staff in the study, a stratified sample was taken using a different sampling fraction for each group of staff. Managers, field social work staff, men and black staff were over-sampled, resulting in an overall sampling fraction of 40% of men and 14% of women; 33% of black staff and 16% of white staff; 43% of managers, 23% of field social work staff, 11% of home care workers and 16% of residential workers (see Table 1.1 for details of the sampling fractions for each authority). Over-sampling ensured sufficient numbers of men and black staff in all job types except home care to allow comparisons and analyses to be made. However, to ensure the reported figures reflected the local authorities and not the sample, weighted data were used.

The interview schedule was based on 50 in-depth interviews carried out in 1992 with representatives of the four job types in a range of authorities other than those where the main study took place. The fully structured questionnaire was divided between a longer interview section, including a work history questionnaire, and a shorter self-completion section. In the course of the first, main interview, respondents were asked about their employment history, their current job, qualifications and training, their feelings about the work, experience of violence and discrimination; their health, personal and domestic situations; and their plans for the future. In the self-completion questionnaire respondents were asked to give further information about their experience of discrimination and to complete the General Health Questionnaire (GHQ). Many of the questions in the interview, and the use of the GHQ, were chosen so that the results of the study would be comparable with the findings from the British Household Panel Survey (Buck et al, 1994). For the second interview, the structure of the first questionnaire was maintained, but job or activity changes after the first interview were recorded and the self-completion questionnaire was shortened. New questions and sections were inserted where it was thought that information gathered in the first interviews might be expanded upon or clarified. These included areas such as caring responsibilities, incidences of violence and racism, methods of learning, income and pensions, and reasons for seeking to change, or not change, one's job.

Both first and second interviews were carried out by Social and Community Planning Research (SCPR). The first interviews took place between September 1993 and February 1994 and the second, after almost a two year interval, between October and December 1995. Of the 1,276 staff interviewed on the first occasion, 940, 74%, were re-interviewed, all of whom were still working for their original social services department, though not necessarily in the same job (see Table 1.2, p 18). About a quarter of the staff who had left were traced and interviewed by telephone. Findings from these interviews are described in Chapter Nine. Most of this book is based, however, on the evidence from those who were interviewed twice in England, Scotland and Northern Ireland.

Scotland

In 1995, there were 39,038 (WTE) staff employed in social work departments in Scotland. The philosophy and content of social work is similar to that practised in England but there are differences both in its

ıe legislation by which it is governed (Fabb and Guthrie,
8). The foundations of the Scottish social work system
966 White Paper on Social Work and the Community
the establishment of comprehensive social work
ṣ proposal led to the 1968 Social Work (Scotland) Act.
The first social work departments in Scottish councils were set up in
1969, replacing the services previously carried out by children's, welfare
and probation departments. The 1968 Act placed on councils very wide
responsibilities for social welfare, including childcare, child protection,
services for families, older people, people with physical or mental disabilities
and for both young and adult offenders. Generic social work was therefore
introduced into Scotland slightly earlier than in England. The Scottish
system differed from the English in that work with offenders became an
integral function of social work departments.

The 1968 Act also made provision for the establishment of the Children's
Hearing system in 1971. This is unique to Scotland and deals with children
under 16 who are in need of care and attention. Such children may have
committed an offence or may be the victim of abuse or neglect. The
welfare of the child is paramount at all Children's Hearings. All referrals
must be made to the Reporter, a full-time official who decides whether
the child should be brought to a Hearing. The Hearing is composed of
three panel members who make the final decision of the appropriate
needs of the child and measures of care required. Panel members are
volunteers drawn from a wide range of backgrounds who have undergone
special training.

The 1995 Children (Scotland) Act is now the key legislation concerning
children, young people and their families. It has been described as the
Scottish equivalent of the 1989 Children Act in England and Wales (Tisdall,
1997). While there are many similarities and 'children in need' is a category
found across UK legislation, there are important differences in both detail
and context. The 1995 Act was fully implemented from April 1998.

Community Care in Scotland is mainly governed by the same
legislation as in England – the 1990 NHS and Community Care Act.
This Act, which aimed to shift the balance of care for vulnerable groups
away from institutional care, resulted in important changes in the way in
which social work services were delivered. It also encouraged a return to
greater specialism in social work.

In 1991 the Scottish Office set National Standards and Objectives for
social work in criminal justice and since that time the bulk of social work
with this user group has been exclusively funded by central government

although practitioners continue to be employed by social work departments. The 1995 Criminal Procedure (Scotland) Act introduced supervised attendance orders providing new duties for social workers and further changes will result from the implementation of the 1997 Crime and Punishment (Scotland) Act.

Local government reorganisation in Scotland

Reorganisation of local government in Scotland followed on from that in Wales. On 1 April 1996, the two tier pattern of Scottish local government was replaced by unitary councils and social work became the responsibility of 32 new authorities instead of 12 regions. The previous structures and terminology were no longer universal and some new councils chose not to have separate social work departments. The first and second interviews for this survey were completed prior to reorganisation, but it might be assumed that its impact would have been felt in advance and would have influenced the study results. There is some evidence, however, that many of the changes affecting the workers in our sample had already taken place. As noted above, there were other legislative changes which were probably of more importance for practitioners. All Scottish social work departments underwent internal reorganisation in the early 1990s. Most, including the two selected, moved from generic teams to specialist social work teams in which work with children and families and work with offenders were separated from work with adults in need of community care. The community care reforms acted as a spur to major changes in structure which had mostly taken place prior to their implementation in 1993 (Buglass, 1993).

Reviewing the experience of the first year of the unitary authorities, Carlisle (1997) noted that changes had been mainly at the top rather than in front-line services and quoted Denise Platt, then Under Secretary for Social Services at the Association of Metropolitan Authorities: "It's in the second year that changes will begin to be felt as authorities begin to realise the nature of their budgets and the services they can provide. But in the first year it will be a measure of success if social workers don't notice." It is likely, therefore, that although the survey took place during a time of great change, the structural impact of local government was less important than the many other alterations to the content and practice of social work.

The Scottish sample

It was intended that the Scottish sample should be comparable with that obtained from England and Northern Ireland. When the study took place social work was a regional responsibility. For the purposes of the study two regions were selected and within each of these regions a social work district was identified from which the sample was selected. Both the study areas were located in urban areas and both contained a mix of deprivation and relative affluence. The first study area, the 'east' social work district, had a population of over 110,000. In comparison with the rest of that region it had a higher proportion of older people and a relatively low proportion of children and young persons. It had, however, a particularly high proportion of young adults, many of whom were students. The second study area, the 'west' social work district, had a population of 275,000 with an age structure similar to the region as a whole. Its population included about 7% from ethnic minorities, mainly from the Indian sub-continent.

The interview schedules used in Scotland were as similar as possible to those used in England but the different legislation and some differences of terminology led to minor modifications. At the time of the study, what were social services departments in England were called social work departments in Scotland. This raised difficulties in relation to the term 'social work staff' which north of the Border can be interpreted as referring to all employees of a social work department. The term 'field social work staff' has therefore been adopted in this book to refer to that group of staff which consisted mainly of qualified social workers but which also included project workers, community workers, counsellors, social work assistants and community care assistants. The 'manager' category contained a broad range of job titles and included higher level management such as district, area and service provision manager, officer in charge, home care supervisor and home care organiser. The 'home care worker' category included home helps and home makers and the 'residential worker' category included all residential staff from deputy officer in charge downwards and some sheltered housing wardens.

The planned size of the Scottish sample was 400 individuals, large enough to ensure that 300 respondents would be available for interview on the second occasion. The sample was selected from personnel records of the two study areas, stratified by local authority, job type and gender (see Table 1.1, p 17 for details of the sampling fractions for each district). Unfortunately both authorities had only recently begun to record the ethnic origin of their employees and it was not possible to use ethnicity as a criterion for selection as was done in England. Only five individuals from ethnic minorities were selected randomly, a number too small from which to draw any conclusions. The number of staff in the four job types and the numbers in each district who took part in the first interview are given in Table 1.1.

The first interviews were carried out by SCPR between June 1994 and the end of February 1995. The total number of interviews was 393. The second interviews took place between January and March 1996, immediately prior to local government reorganisation. Thus the average interval between the first and second interviews of 15 months was shorter than that in England. Of the 393 people interviewed in Scotland in the first round 317, or 81%, were re-interviewed.

Northern Ireland

In October 1973, the delivery of hospital, family practitioner services, community health services and personal social services was delegated by government to four Health and Social Services Boards based on geographical areas of the Province, and to other relevant agencies. The services were planned and managed both at Board and District level by a corporate management system which integrated health and social services, though at delivery level there was considerable separation between different elements of health and social services. Over the following period, this structure largely remained intact, though in the late 1980s there was a move from corporate management to a general management system, with one chief executive, initially at Board level, but rapidly followed at District level, with professional advice available from the senior staff of each discipline. When 'Working for patients' was published by the Department of Health in January, 1989, the then Northern Ireland Minister for Health and Social Services stressed its importance for Northern Ireland. The Health and Personal Social Services (Northern Ireland) Order followed in 1991, introducing fundamental changes in the organisation and management of health and personal social services in Northern Ireland. Boards, instead of having responsibility for service management, were to become primarily responsible for assessing the health and social care needs of the population, while Directly Managed Units, which replaced District organisations, provided services to meet those needs, along with services purchased from the voluntary and private sectors. It was anticipated that some of the Directly Managed Units were likely to be established as Health and Social Services Trusts, which would be set up as separate legal entities within the health and social service system. A new set of contractual arrangements would form the linkage between Trusts and purchasing Boards. In the event, at the time of the first workforce interviews, one Board – the Eastern Health and Social Services Board, had already been organised into separate Trusts, including four which were primarily concerned with the provision of personal social services. Government, influenced by the development of NHS Trusts in Great Britain, then decided that, from April 1996, all services in Northern Ireland should be provided by Health and Social Services Trusts, including the responsibility for statutory powers such as those under the 1968 Children and Young Persons Act, replaced by the 1995 Children (Northern Ireland) Order, and the 1986 Mental Health (Northern Ireland) Order. Thus, when the second interviews were taking place, the final arrangements were being made and staff appointed to their new responsibilities to their Trust employers.

Health and Social Service Trusts had considerable freedom to devise their own management systems. In some Trusts, services were restructured on a service user basis, and managed in an interdisciplinary way. For example, the mental health team could consist of a range of mental health specialists – including nurses, psychiatrists, psychologists, occupational therapists and social workers – while the team would be led by the person appointed to the post, from whatever background they came. For social work staff the break between managerial supervision and professional supervision was a new, and unsettling departure from traditional forms of supervision.

The survey took place, like all other events in Northern Ireland, against the back-drop of the 'Troubles'. While no Board area was exempt from the impact of current events, it is important to remember that, in many areas, the impact on day-to-day life was felt less than in others. The first interviews took place as the two cease-fires were beginning to have an effect. While the second interviews were taking place, the first IRA cease-fire came to an end.

The Northern Ireland sample

In Northern Ireland, partly because of the relatively small scale of the population, but also because of the willingness of all four Boards to be involved, the survey covered statutory social services throughout the Province. Thus in Northern Ireland, unlike in England and Scotland, we drew a national sample from all statutory and service providers and agencies.

While it was intended that the Northern Ireland sample should be broadly comparable with those in England and Scotland, inevitably some differences emerged. The original intention was to sample 400 staff with equal numbers in each of the four job types and the sample approximating to about 10% of each staff group. However, Northern Ireland has a much larger percentage of home care workers than England and Scotland and a sample of 10% of these would have resulted in a sample over 400. In the event, it was decided to include 1% of the home care workers, compared with approximately 12% of the other three job types and for most purposes to analyse them separately from managers, field social work staff and residential workers. Care has therefore been exercised in comparing Northern Ireland results with those from England and Scotland and the reader will find Northern Ireland home care staff omitted from some composite tables and considered separately.

Men and people from minority ethnic groups were over-sampled in the English survey. While gender was known from the staff listings in Northern Ireland, the fact that the sample had to be hand drawn obviated against making a distinction on grounds of gender, and the sample was stratified only by Board and job type (see Table 1.1, p 17 for details of the sampling fractions for each Board). Information on ethnicity was not available in the Northern Ireland records and no minority ethnic group members were in the panel.

Two further features distinguished the Northern Ireland survey. Firstly, the Social Services Inspectorate in Northern Ireland, and representatives of the Boards on the Advisory Group, were particularly interested in information about residential social work staff in childcare. As a result, it was decided to sample childcare workers only. Because job titles were not unique to childcare staff, however, residential workers and care assistants working with other user groups were inadvertently selected. The sample of residential workers in Northern Ireland therefore included these and supervisory staff from residential facilities with all user groups, but mainly those working with people with learning difficulties and those with mental health problems.

Secondly, a special section was added to the self-completion questionnaire in which Northern Ireland respondents were asked about their community identification and the extent of perceived discrimination on grounds of community identity they experienced in the course of their current jobs. The findings from these questions are considered in

Chapter Six alongside the experiences of racial and other discrimination reported in the English survey.

Interviews were carried out in Northern Ireland between October 1994 and January 1995 and January and March 1996 by what was then known as the Policy Planning Research Unit. The interval between interviews was similar to that for Scotland, on average about 15 months. Three hundred and sixty-two staff were interviewed on the first occasion and 316 on the second, 88% of the original sample. The numbers of staff in the four job types and the numbers who took part in the first interview in each Board are given in Table 1.1.

Characteristics of the three studies

Table 1.1 gives details of the total number of staff in the job types of manager, field social work staff, home care worker and residential worker who were employed in the five social services departments in England in 1993-94, and in the social work departments in Scotland and Boards in Northern Ireland in 1994-95. The second column gives the total numbers of staff in each department or Board who took part in the first interview; the third column gives the sampling fraction, that is, the percentage of staff interviewed as a proportion of the total number.

Allowing for the slight discrepancy caused by the sampling of Northern Ireland home care workers, broadly similar proportions of staff in each department or Board took part in the first interviews.

Table 1.2 gives the distribution of staff in each of the main categories examined throughout this book. Proportions are given for each study and are based on unweighted data. Percentages may differ from those elsewhere in the book and in other published material, which, in order to estimate attributes of the workforce population, are mostly based on weighted data (or *Base* numbers).

Table 1.1: First interview: numbers of staff in each department or Board and sampling fractions

Department or Board	Total employed	Total interviewed	Sampling fraction (%)
England			
Outer London borough A	855	185	22
Midlands metropolitan borough council B	1,479	272	18
County council C	1,855	269	15
Northern metropolitan borough council D	2,149	324	15
Inner London borough E	1,003	226	22
Total		**1,276**	
Scotland			
East social work district	879	198	22
West social work district	2,179	195	9
Total		**393**	
Northern Ireland *			
Eastern Health & Social Services Board	4,644	157	3
Northern Health & Social Services Board	2,542	78	3
Southern Health & Social Services Board	3,260	76	2
Western Health & Social Services Board	2,081	51	2
Total		**362**	

* Note: excluding home care workers in Northern Ireland increases the sampling fraction for the other three job types to 12%.

Table 1.2 shows that women predominated in each study, the highest proportion being in Northern Ireland. Staff aged less than 30 were in a minority; a slightly higher proportion of the Northern Ireland sample were aged 30 to 39, and a quarter of each sample were aged 50 or over. As already described, men were over-sampled in England and Scotland, black staff were over-sampled in England and managers and field social work staff were over-sampled in all three studies to allow comparisons to be made, and a sample weighting was applied to the data when estimating the attributes of the population.

Table 1.2: First interview: percentage distribution of staff in each of the three studies

	England	Scotland	Northern Ireland
Gender			
Women	68	69	83
Men	32	31	17
Ethnic group			
Black	17	1	–
White	83	99	–
Community identification			
Catholic	–	–	44
Protestant	–	–	36
Other/neither	–	–	17
Age at first interview			
Less than 30	10	9	8
30 to 39	28	32	40
40 to 49	37	33	29
50 or over	26	25	23
Job type			
Manager	25	18	22
Field social work staff	18	28	33
Home care worker	28	30	19
Residential worker	29	25	25
Employer			
Outer London borough A	15	East 50	East 43
Midlands metropolitan borough council B	21	West 50	North 22
County council C	21		South 21
North metropolitan borough council D	25		West 14
Inner London borough E	18		
Number of first interviews	**1,276**	**393**	**362**

Table 1.3 shows the proportions of staff who were interviewed a second time. Differences in follow-up rates were entirely related to the sample in each department or Board, and cannot be taken to be representative; the purpose of including this information is to give a general idea of the proportions of staff who were interviewed a second time. Again, percentages are based on unweighted data, and may differ slightly from those quoted elsewhere.

Table 1.3: Percentages of staff in each sample interviewed a second time

	England		Scotland		Northern Ireland
Whole sample	74		81		88
Gender					
Women	74		79		87
Men	74		85		95
Ethnic group					
Black	64		100		–
White	76		80		–
Community identification					
Catholic	–		–		90
Protestant	–		–		90
Other/neither	–		–		84
Age at first interview					
Less than 30	63		81		80
30 to 39	73		79		92
40 to 49	83		89		91
50 or over	67		73		82
Job type					
Manager	79		90		94
Field social work staff	82		83		92
Home care worker	71		71		77
Residential worker	66		83		88
Employer					
Outer London borough A	68	East	80	East	91
Midlands metropolitan borough council B	73	West	82	North	85
County Council C	79			South	88
North metropolitan borough council D	78			West	86
Inner London borough E	66				
Number of second interviews	**940**		**317**		**316**
Number of first interviews	1,276		393		362

A lower proportion of staff in England were followed up than in Scotland or Northern Ireland. This may have been due to differences in the time between interviews, which in England averaged just under two years, whereas in Scotland and Northern Ireland, it was about 15 months. Fewer home care workers than staff in any other job type were interviewed a second time, partly because they were often extremely difficult to contact, being predominantly part-time and not office-based. The lower follow-up of home care workers accounts for the lower follow-up rate among other categories of staff, particularly women (home care workers are mostly women). In each study, a higher proportion of managers and field social work staff were interviewed twice, which partly accounts for the higher proportion of men who were followed up. Further discussion of staff who left the study is contained in Chapter Nine.

Much of the discussion in subsequent chapters compares the experiences of women and men, and Table 1.4 provides a summary of the proportions of women and men in each job type at the first and second interviews. Because comparisons are being made between women and men, weighted data are used.

Table 1.4: Percentages of women and men in each job type at the first and second interviews

	England		Scotland		Northern Ireland*	
	Women	**Men**	**Women**	**Men**	**Women**	**Men**
First interview						
Whole sample	86	14	89	11	78	22
Manager	65	35	65	35	71	30
Field social work staff	78	22	71	29	77	23
Home care worker	96	4	99	<1	100	0
Residential worker	85	15	83	17	89	11
Base	807	127	351	42	225*	62
Second interview						
Whole sample	86	14	88	12	78	22
Manager	67	33	66	34	61	39
Field social work staff	77	23	73	27	81	19
Home care worker	97	3	99	1	100	0
Residential worker	88	12	86	15	91	9
Base	573	91	266	36	204*	59

* *Base* numbers exclude 70 (unweighted [unw]) Northern Ireland home care workers who were all women.

The table shows a common pattern in each study of women predominating in each job type, with higher proportions of men in jobs as managers. The distribution of women and men at the first interview was maintained at the second interview.

Outline of the book

Chapter Two focuses on how people enter social care work, exploring routes into social care from the work history data. It looks at age of entry, previous types of employment, exits from and returns to social care work and numbers of jobs held within the social services. It provides a general understanding of workforce dynamics and specific underpinning for the discussion of careers in Chapters Seven and Nine.

Chapter Three describes the responsibilities and tasks undertaken by social services staff. Drawing on the second interviews, it shows how the introduction of new arrangements for providing community care and other changes have affected duties and daily routine. It considers the extent to which the work of social services staff has changed, with an increase in time spent on administration and a reduction in the time spent in face-to-face contact with users.

Chapter Four evaluates staff's experience of job satisfaction and stress at work. It analyses the complex relationships between stress, role conflict, job satisfaction and time off sick, which were broadly similar in the three studies. It outlines constructive and positive policies that employers could follow to increase job satisfaction and reduce stress.

Chapter Five examines the violence which those who work in the social services experience in the course of their work. It includes evidence from both the social services and comparable professions such as the police and health services. Violence at work can take many forms, from serious physical attacks to verbal abuse and harassment. The chapter shows how the risk of violence varies according to job type, gender, age and other characteristics. It concludes with a discussion of the law relating to violence at work and of the different responses that have been developed.

Chapter Six discusses the distribution of staff between job types by ethnic group and gender, the views of social services staff on equal opportunities policies and how social services departments put these into practice. It looks in particular at black staff in England who experienced racism from service users and their relatives and from colleagues and managers. Evidence on community identification and discrimination in Northern Ireland is also considered. Overall, the chapter reviews the different forms of discrimination in the workplace and the consequences of these for staff, employers and service users.

Chapter Seven explores women's under-representation in social services management. Drawing on the work histories, it illustrates how women's careers have been disadvantaged by part-time working, limited job mobility and a relative lack of educational and professional qualifications. It suggests policies to pursue more effective equal opportunities in the future.

In response to concern over standards of practice, training for social work and social care has seen major investment and change in the 1990s. Chapter Eight looks at how developments in training have affected the workforce. It argues that a continuum of education and training for all staff should assume priority during a period of rapid change in which the inherited skills and attitudes of the workforce may not always be appropriate. Training may facilitate job mobility, but employers should view this positively in a workforce with a relatively low staff turnover.

Chapter Nine looks at job changes during the period between the two interviews. It considers the characteristics of those who changed jobs, but remained within their social services/social work department, as well as those who left. Drawing on telephone interviews with leavers, it includes verbatim comments from those interviewed to illustrate some of the factors, mainly associated with job dissatisfaction, which encourage people to move.

Chapter Ten, in conclusion, explores the significance of the similarities and differences between the three samples. It extends the discussion of the main issues highlighted by the research and relates them to the different perspectives of service users, employers and staff. It endorses the commitment and expertise of a workforce faced with changes on many fronts and defines those policies and practices which might support the continuation of its strengths while preparing it to meet the challenges of the future.

TWO

Employment history of social services staff

Toby Andrew

Introduction

Large organisations acquire their workforce over time, and that workforce becomes both a central strength and a potential obstacle to change. As organisations move into new areas of service, the skills, knowledge and values of the workforce may lag behind. The ability of service organisations to retain and re-educate their workforce for new agendas is, therefore, fundamental to their successful delivery of new services. In turn this depends on knowledge of the work histories of staff and their previous work experience and training. This chapter introduces the information collected on the work histories of staff in our three samples and shows how an understanding of these retrospective studies can contribute to the workforce's future development.

The Workforce studies included the collection of a retrospective work history from 2,031 staff in England, Scotland and Northern Ireland at the first interview in 1994-95. Staff were asked to recall in some detail every job or other activity they had performed that had lasted for a month or more (such as training, looking after the home, maternity leave and unemployment), beginning with the first job in social care. In addition staff were asked about their work experience prior to their first job in social care. The work history did not record more than one activity at a time, such as holding a second job or attending a day-release course. Secondments were treated as a period of training, rather than a period of employment. (For details of the work history data collection, see Ginn et al, 1997.)

The work history for staff ranged as far back as 1951 for one member, to within 12 months of the first interview for 29 others. The retrospective data on previous social care work recorded in which sector the job had been held (for example, statutory, voluntary or private), the work setting, the user group, employment conditions and the responsibilities of the post. A distinction was made as to whether a social care job was held in social services or elsewhere. Any activity that did not involve work in social care was recorded as full- or part-time work, unemployment, maternity leave, looking after family, full-time education, training or some other activity. Despite some of the inaccuracies that recall data involves (Dex, 1991), the dataset provides us with a unique profile of the working lives of the social services workforce in 11 local authorities and Boards in the United Kingdom of Great Britain and Northern Ireland.

Most figures in this chapter are reported separately for each of the three samples, but where no significant differences are detected between them, pooled figures across the three studies are presented instead. However, it must be emphasised that such pooled figures represent the areas surveyed and cannot be considered to be representative of the whole of the UK.

Work experience prior to working in social care

When considering the acquired skills of the workforce it is useful to consider the background of staff and their experience outside of social services, in addition to any formal qualifications held.

About 80% of staff in all three samples reported they had held paid work prior to their first job in social care. Almost all home care workers (95%) had previously held a paid job or had been self-employed before their first job in social care, as had about 70% of managers and field social work staff. This is not surprising since on average managers, social work staff and residential workers took the first job in social care in their late twenties, while home care workers did so in their mid-thirties.

Younger staff in management, social work and residential work were less likely to have been employed before taking up social care work. About 60% of staff who were under 40 years old at first interview had held a previous job compared with about 80% of those who were 40 or over. Home care workers of all ages were equally likely to have held employment before social care.

There was little or no difference between the proportions of women and men citing work experience prior to social care. Women and men who had worked prior to their first social care job did differ, however, in the type of work that they had previously carried out. This was particularly true of staff in management and social work and is illustrated in Figure 2.1 below. In all three samples women were more likely than men in management and social work to have been previously employed in clerical work (45% compared with 20%) or sales (12% compared with 6%), while men in management and social work were more likely than women to have been employed in management or a professional job (19% compared with 10%), craft or related work (16% compared with 1%), or plant/machine operations or unskilled manual work (15% compared with 5%). A similar pattern of employment emerged for residential workers and home care workers, although there was no distinction in residential work between the proportions of women and men previously employed in manual work.

Figure 2.1: Employment prior to first job in social care for women and men in management and social work at first interview

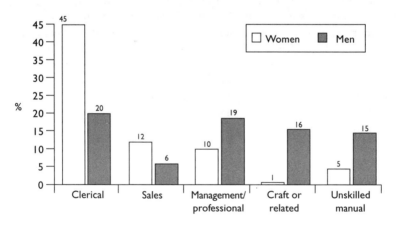

The most common type of employment before social care was with a private company (about 55% of all staff), the health service (11%) or a local authority or education board (9%). Eighteen per cent of staff had no previous employment. In all four social service job types included in the study, women were more likely than men to have been previously employed by the health service, while in some cases men were more likely than women to have been employed by a private firm. A striking exception to the latter were home care workers in Northern Ireland, all of whom were women and 78% of whom had worked in a private firm before taking their first job in social care.

There is therefore a relationship between social services and other employers. In some cases, private business gave the social services workforce its first experience of work, and private companies may have contributed to training the future social services workforce. The health service, too, appears to have played a role in giving social services staff initial work experience. What remains unclear is whether this initial experience is subsequently of value in social services work.

Social care employment before entering the statutory social services

For the majority of the workforce a job in social services was the first experience of working in social care. In England and Northern Ireland this was the case for three quarters of the workforce, while in Scotland 85% of staff had taken their first social care job in a social work department. In all three samples home care workers were the most likely to have taken their first social care job in social services (about 90%).

In most cases there was no difference between women and men in the proportions who reported having previously worked in social care before joining social services. The exception to this was in Northern Ireland, where men in management and social work were more likely to have been employed in social care before entering social services (45% compared to 21% of women) and in Scotland, where women social work staff were more likely to have done so than men (36% and 21% respectively). Younger staff in home care and residential work were more likely to have been employed in social care before entering social services. About 30% of home care workers and residential workers under 40 years of age had been previously employed in social care compared with about 10% over 40. This was not the case for managers and social work staff.

One in ten of the workforce said they had been employed in social care prior to the establishment of social services departments (SSDs) in 1971 (1969 in Scotland). Prior to 1971, three quarters of this group of staff had worked for a local authority, a quarter in a hospital setting or for the NHS, a tenth for a voluntary or community work organisation and a tenth in the private sector. The implications of these experiences prior to working in social services are explored in Chapter Eight.

Age at key events

People did not generally join social services until after they had substantial experience of adult life. For example, women who were employed in field social work in England on average began work in social services at the age of 30 years. The age of first employment in social services ranged between 17 and 47 years for 95% of these staff. In Scotland and Northern Ireland, women employed in social work at first interview tended to join social services a little younger, on average at 27-28 years (ranging between 18 and 44). Table 2.1 gives pooled figures for age of entry for the three studies. Male social work staff in all three studies joined social services at the same age of about 28, ranging between 18 and 43 years.

On the other hand, among managers at first interview in England, men had first joined social services at a younger age than women (27 compared with women at the age of 30). Table 2.1 also shows the pooled average for the three studies for the ages at which key events in early career development took place. The table shows that for all three studies women were significantly older than men in residential work at interview and on first joining social services.

Table 2.1: Age at key events for staff in England, Scotland and Northern Ireland

	Manager		Social work staff		Home care		Residential	
Mean age at:	Women	Men	Women	Men	Women	Men	Women	Men
First social care job	27	25	27	26	36	38	30*	28
First social services job	29	27	29	28	37	40	32*	29
Qualifying training	31	30	30	30	-	-	36	[34]
First interview (1994/95)	43	42	40	39	47	45	43*	36
Base	*136*	*68*	*264*	*81*	*669*	*17*	*385*	*65*
n	254	213	306	164	496	47	390	161

* Difference between women and men statistically significant at p < 0.05.

[ ] indicates calculation is based upon less than 20 people and is therefore an unreliable estimate.

Figures in this table are approximate, since there are variations in age between countries.

Total number of years employed by social services

Experience is a major asset in any workforce, but perhaps especially where the workforce is dealing with complex human dilemmas and where the personal qualities of each worker can significantly influence the effectiveness of the service. Once embarked on a career in social services, people tended to have substantial periods of service. In each study, staff had been employed in social services on average for a total of 10 years (Figure 2.2), for most staff ranging between one and 23 years. The figure of 10 years does not include any time staff may have spent outside the employment of social services, such as looking after family or in full-time education.

Figure 2.2 Average number of years employed by social services: years by gender and job type at first interview

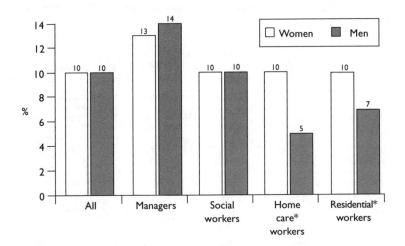

* The total number of years worked in social services by women home care and residential workers in all three studiess was significantly longer than men.

Staff who had worked longest in social services were managers and naturally tended to be older. In England white staff had worked in social services longer than black staff (on average 10 years compared with seven), except in residential work where there was no difference in length of employment. Here black and white residential workers had been employed by social services for an average of nine years.

Although there was no overall difference in length of service between women and men, there was a significant difference between women and men in different job types. Figure 2.2 illustrates for all three studies a similar length of service for women and men in management and field social work and the differences in home care and residential work, where women were employed longer than men.

The general picture was that women and men in social work were of similar ages, had been employed by social services for a total of about 10 years and qualified at similar ages. In management a similar pattern emerged, except that all managers had been employed in social services in total for longer and male managers tended to join social services at a younger age than women.

On the other hand, in residential work men were younger than women at first interview, had joined social services at a younger age and had worked for less time in social services. Men in home care had also worked for less time in social services compared with women, but there were no significant age differences, either at the first interview or on first joining social services.

Number of jobs held and rate of job change in social services

Younger staff were most likely to record the highest job turnover in social services. On average job turnover for staff under 30 was about 7 jobs per decade, for staff in their thirties, 5 jobs per decade, in their forties, 3 jobs per decade and staff 50 or over, 2 jobs every decade. The higher job turnover among younger staff to some extent may reflect the fact that they did not have to recollect so far back in time in reporting their work history and may have been more likely to recall short spells of employment (see Dex, 1991). However, we did find that younger staff were also more likely than older staff to have moved jobs between interviews after a two year follow-up period (see Chapter Nine).

The past rate of job change differed according to the four job types at first interview. Home care workers had the lowest past turnover of jobs (about 3 jobs per decade) compared with managers, social work staff and residential workers (about 4 jobs per decade, see Table 2.2).

In addition to the differences in past mobility between job types, there were also differences in mobility between women and men home care and residential workers. Figure 2.3 seems to suggest that on average men across all job types held roughly 5 jobs every decade, compared with less than 4 per decade for women (first two columns). On closer inspection however, this gender difference was only true for home care and residential workers. In home care and residential work, men had not only joined social services more recently than women (Figure 2.2), but also had a higher rate of job change in social services (Figure 2.3). Men and women in management and field social work had almost identical rates of job change (a grand average of about 4 jobs per decade), while for men working in home care and residential work, the average turnover was 6 jobs every decade – exactly twice the turnover for women in this work.

Table 2.2: Rate of past job turnover per decade by job type and age at first interview in England, Scotland and Northern Ireland

Turnover per decade	Job type	Base	n	Age		Base	n
Manager	3.8	204	467	Under 30	7.1*	154	189
Social work staff	4.6	345	470	30-39	5.1	463	620
Home care	2.7*	686	543	40-49	2.9	555	702
Residential	4.3	450	551	50 +	2.1	505	513
All	3.6	1,685	2,031			1,677	2,024

*Job turnover was lower for home care workers and older members of staff. Significant at $p < 0.05$, controlling for gender and regional variations.

Although job turnover within social services only differed between home care workers and other staff, the *type* of movement made by staff was different. Managers and social work staff were more likely to make 'career-related' job moves or move in and out of social services than home care and residential workers (Ginn et al, 1997). The term 'career-related' job move is used here in a loose sense as an indication of types of past movement, since the moves considered include not only those between different types of work – between management, field social work, home care, residential work and other social care work – but also in and out of social services, which could have been for training, full-time education, family reasons or employment in work other than social care. Defined in this way, a 'career-related' move may have negative as well as positive effects upon the careers of staff.

Figure 2.3 Average number of jobs held per decade of employment in social services for staff in England, Scotland and Northern Ireland

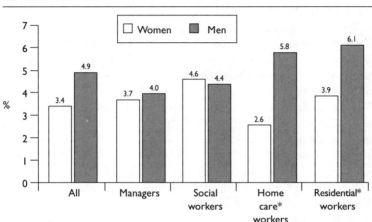

* Denotes men in home and residential care have a higher job turnover than women. Analysis of variance significant at $p<0.05$ controlling for age and regional variations.

There was no overall difference, for any of the four job types in any of the three samples, between the incidence of women and men moving either between different types of work or moving in and out of social services. However, field social work staff and managers made these moves more often than home care or residential staff. About 80% of managers and 60% of social work staff had made such a move since first joining social services, compared with only 14% of home care and 37% of residential workers. What did differ for men and women, was why they left social services. As explained below, women were more likely to take a break for family-related reasons, while men were more likely to take (mostly unpaid) qualifying training.

Past activity outside social services since first joining social services

A career in social services did not mean an unbroken period of service. Just under a quarter of staff had left and rejoined social services at least once since first taking a job in social services. This varied between job types with 40% of managers and field social work staff, 10% of home care workers and 23% of residential workers having done so. Older staff in management and field social work were more likely to have left and returned, while the opposite was true for residential workers, with younger residential workers being more likely to have left and returned.

The main reasons cited for temporarily leaving were in order to undertake training or full-time education (12% of the workforce rising to about 40% of men in management and social work); to look after the family or take maternity leave (about 10% of the workforce – rising to just under 20% of women managers and social work staff); employment in work unrelated to social care or a spell of unemployment (8%, rising to 12% among social work staff and residential workers); social care employment outside social services (6%, rising to 10% among managers and social work staff) and other unrelated activities such as travelling abroad (2% of the workforce, rising to 5% of social work staff and staff under 30). The figures cited above total more than a quarter, because, of those who had left and rejoined social services, about a third had done so more than once.

Men, particularly those in their forties, were more likely than women to have reported a period of qualifying training – mainly unpaid – or to have attended full-time education. This reflected the fact that, compared with women in management and social work, men were more likely to hold a social work qualification.

Women in management and social work at first interview were more likely to have reported taking maternity leave or time out to look after the family compared with women in home care and residential work (15% compared with 7%), but home care and residential workers were more likely throughout their work history to have been employed part-time. Having previously left social services to look after family members was most common among women in their thirties and forties at first interview.

Qualifying training

Given the often substantial prior experience of work among the workforce, were social services employers recruiting staff with appropriate qualifications, or was it necessary to train staff subsequently? Most staff who held a social work qualification at first interview (Diploma in Social Work [DipSW], Certificate of Qualification in Social Work [CQSW] or Certificate in Social Services [CSS]), had obtained it after first joining social services. About 62% of staff with a social work qualification had become qualified after joining social services, 26% qualified in the same year as joining and 12% qualified before joining. This varied across the three samples with three quarters of staff in England qualifying after joining compared with over half in Scotland and Northern Ireland. Twenty-one per cent of staff had qualified in the 1970s (or earlier), 53% in the 1980s and 26% in the 1990s.

On average staff became qualified about four years after first joining social services, ranging from seven years before their first job in social services to 17 years after. There were variations by the year they qualified, where they worked and the type of job they held at first interview. Staff who qualified in the 1990s did so before or when they first joined social services, while those who qualified in the 1980s or earlier, were more likely to have qualified after joining social services. In England staff qualified on average five years after joining social services, while in Scotland and Northern Ireland staff qualified sooner, on average two-and-a-half years after joining. Field social workers at first interview were more likely than qualified managers and residential workers to have qualified before joining social services.

Table 2.3 below illustrates that in the 1990s social workers from all three samples were more likely to qualify before their first job in social services compared with those who qualified in the 1980s and 1970s.

Table 2.3: Percentages of qualified social workers at first interview who qualified before their first job in social services

	1970s (or earlier)	1980s	1990s
Qualified social worker	17	48	91
Base	*98*	*120*	*42*
n	131	175	52

There were no differences in the proportions of women and men who had qualified before working in social services. Overall, however, women were less likely to be qualified than men. At first interview, 51% of women managers held a CQSW, DipSW or CSS qualification compared with 77% of men, while among social work staff, 73% of women were qualified compared with 85% of men.

Work and family life

An experienced workforce is likely to contain people with substantial family commitments, particularly if the workforce is predominantly female. In the three studies, well over 80% of the workforce were women. About 55% of senior social workers, team leaders and middle management were women. The majority of staff reported having dependent children living with them either at the time of their first job in social care (50%) or after this (20%). The remainder had either never had children or had raised them to the age of 16 years before taking their first job in social care. Whether staff had dependent children or not after joining social care, varied by the type of job held at first interview and gender.

In all three samples home care workers were more likely to have had dependent children at the time of their first job in social care, but after this were far less likely to have dependent children compared with other staff. On average about 5% of all home care workers reported having dependent children after their first social care job, compared with over a third of managers and field social work staff and about 20% of residential workers.

Women in management and field social work were less likely than men to have dependent children after their first job in social care. Just under a third of women managers had dependent children after their first job in social care compared with 60% of men. In terms of taking unpaid leave to care for children and family, women in social services were primarily responsible for childcare (Table 2.4). It is likely for this reason that fewer women in management had children compared with men, which suggests in turn that childcare is a limitation on the career progress of women (see Chapter Seven). This was also the case among social work staff, with only a third of women reporting having had dependent children after their first job in social care, compared with half of men. There were no significant differences in the incidence of having dependent children for women and men in home care and residential work.

Table 2.4: Past periods of non-employment since first job in social services by gender and job type

	Manager		Social work staff		Home care		Residential	
	W	M	W	M	W	M	W	M
Mean length of break (years):								
Maternity leave	1.1	-	0.8	-	0.6	-	1.0	-
Family care	3.2	-	6.1	-	4.5	-	3.1	-
Unemployment	[0.5]	[0.5]	[0.8]	[0.5]	[0.4]	-	0.5	0.4
% taking break for:								
Maternity leave	4	-	7	-	1	-	3	-
Family care	13*	0	14*	0	8	-	10	0
Unemployment	3	6	10	15	4	4	10*	18
Base	*136*	*68*	*264*	*81*	*669*	*17*	*385*	*65*
n	254	213	306	164	496	47	390	161

W = Women M = Men

* Difference between women and men statistically significant at p < 0.05.

[ ] indicates calculation is based upon less than 20 people and is therefore an unreliable estimate.

Table 2.4 details the time spent out of employment for staff in all three studies since their first job in social services. The table shows that only women had spent time caring for the family. About one in 10 women in management and field social work had spent time, on average a total of three and six years respectively, not working since first joining social services in order to look after the home and family. Women social work staff had spent longer out of employment looking after the family than women in other types of work. In home care and residential work, about one in 20 women had spent non-employed time looking after the family, on average for a total of four years.

Surprisingly few women in social services reported taking maternity leave. On average only 3% of women across all four job types reported taking maternity leave, despite the fact that most women staff not only had had children at some point in their lives, but most (55%) had first joined social services under the age of 35 years. For example, a third of women in field social work at first interview, reported having had a baby in a year *after* first joining social services. However, only 7% of these same women reported taking paid maternity leave (Table 2.4). This implies that most women who had a baby while in the employ of social services took unpaid leave to have children. Only about one in five women social work staff who had a baby after joining social services reported taking maternity leave. (For women in management, home care and residential work, the figure was one in six.)

Similar proportions of women and men in management and field social work had spent the same amount of time unemployed, except in Northern Ireland, where fewer women than men in social work reported unemployment. In residential work women in all three studies were less likely to report unemployment than men.

Past movement between social services/social work departments

The majority of staff (87%) had only ever worked for one local authority or Board since first joining social services, although this did vary greatly between the different jobs staff performed at first interview and the type of employer worked for. In general, managers and social work staff were more likely than home care and residential workers to have worked for more than one local authority during their career.

In England, 43% of managers and social work staff had previously been employed by two or three local authorities other than the one in which they were interviewed. In Scotland and Northern Ireland the comparable figures were 25% and 12% respectively, having been employed by one or two other local authorities or Boards.

By contrast, only 2% of home care workers and 11% of residential workers had ever worked for another authority. These staff had previously been employed, on average, by only one other local authority or Board.

Past movement between social care sectors

From the mid–1980s, when the government agenda for social care implied a substantial expansion of the private sector, those employed in social services may have had to consider the prospect of working outside the statutory sector. It is therefore highly relevant that, since first taking a job in social care, less than 15% of workforce time had been spent outside social services. Field social work staff and staff in their thirties had spent the most time (just under 25%) outside social services.

Historically there was very little movement into the private and voluntary sectors *with staff subsequently moving back into social services*. Staff who had permanently left social services are not reflected in our retrospective work history data, since by definition, all staff in the study were in social services at first interview.

As indicated earlier, about 25% of the workforce in England and Northern Ireland had worked in the non-social services care sector before entering social services, while in Scotland the figure was 15%. However, at first interview only 6% of staff had moved to the private or voluntary sector and subsequently returned, since first joining social services (or local authority if prior to 1971). This figure rose to 10% among social work staff and managers.

Typical career pathways for the 1993/94 social services workforce

What kind of careers did social services staff pursue? The majority of staff in our sample had taken their first job in social services in the 1980s (51%), 30% joined in the 1970s or earlier and 19% had joined in the 1990s. The year of entry varied between job types. On average current managers had joined in the late 1970s, while other staff had joined in the early to mid-1980s. Most women and men in home care and residential work had joined in the early 1980s and late 1980s respectively. These findings illustrate a distinctive and unique feature of this workforce, which is, older at entry than others in comparable occupations such as nursing (Beishon et al, 1995). Given the different career paths taken by the different staff at first interview, a brief description is outlined for each job category below.

Strategic and area manager and team leaders

Half of strategic and area management had a background in field social work (50%) and residential work in social services (20%). The remainder had either been in management since first joining social services (20%) or had joined management via other social care work in the social services (10%).

The most common background for field social work team leaders, in descending order, was field social work, residential work and other social care work in the social services. Of the team leaders at first interview, about 70% had originally started in field social work. A minority of these had joined social services as team leaders directly, having first qualified or worked beforehand in the non-statutory social care sector. A fifth of team leaders began in residential work and 10% had originated from other social care jobs in social services. Most of the team leaders who started in social work had worked continuously in field social work, although this did not preclude leaving social services for training, other work or family-related reasons. For staff starting in residential work the most common path to becoming a team leader was via field social work, although a few had come via other types of social care work or became team leaders directly after leaving residential work.

Field social work staff

Most field social work staff had always worked in the field or closely related work since first joining social services. At first interview, about 60% had either been employed in field social work continuously since first joining social services, or also had experience in community work, agency, advice or office-based work. About 20% had started work in residential work, 15% in other social care and 3% first started in home care. In addition, many social work staff had also had experience during their career of social care employment outside social services (38%).

Between entering social services and taking up the social work post at first interview, staff could have taken many different social service jobs, undergone qualifying training, taken a break from social services to care for the family, been employed outside social services and so on. The most common type of career path was starting out in social work, moving between field social work posts (including between team leader and field social work), moving out of social services for training, work or caring for family and subsequently returning as a social worker or team leader. Half of all field social work staff had left social services at least once in their career for one of these reasons. The second most common career path was starting in residential work and moving into social work, often having been an officer in charge or having undergone training.

A typical example of a career in social work might be described as follows. The member of staff joins social services in the mid-1980s as a social work assistant or a residential worker. After a few years she leaves or is seconded to take qualifying training and returns as a qualified social worker. After a couple of jobs in field social work, either before or after training, she may leave for work outside social services, usually in social care (10%) although not always (6%), perhaps has a spell looking after the family (16%) or takes a break from field social work (10%, coded as unemployed or 'other') and finally returns as a social worker.

Of the four job types, field social work staff were most likely to have left social services to do something other than social care work, even when training is not considered. A total of 22% reported having spent time outside of social services since first joining, working in something other than social care or being unemployed. This points to similar evidence from the 1991 Census study of qualified social workers that showed that in 1993, 20% of qualified social workers were working in another field or not working at all (Smyth, 1996). The most common activities pursued by social work staff outside the employment of social services, excluding training and social care work, was looking after the home or family for women (14%), other employment (12%), unemployment (11%), maternity leave (7%) or pursuing some other interest (8%).

Home care organisers and home care workers

Half the home care organisers had always worked in home care. Of the remainder about 20% had started in field social work, 20% in other social care and less than 10% had begun in residential work. The majority of home care workers had always worked in home care (85%). The remaining staff had moved within social services to join home care, primarily via other types of social care work (10%), 3% had started out in residential work and 2% in field social work. A total of about 10% of all home care workers had left social services since first joining, to take up non-social care work or look after the family. This was lower than for the rest of the workforce, of whom more than a fifth had done so.

Officers in charge of residential homes and residential workers

Nine out of ten officers in charge had worked almost continuously in residential work with little past movement between different setting or job. Most of what little movement there was occurred between social work and residential work with about 7% of officers in charge starting out in social work. Three quarters of residential workers had always worked in residential work, 15% had worked in other social care, 7% had started in home care and 2% had started in social work.

Conclusions

One distinguishing feature of the social services workforce has been the late age of entry of staff into social care. As noted earlier, people have not generally joined social services until they have had substantial experience of adult life. Entry in mid or late twenties has been preceded by a wide range of employment in other occupations, providing a rich world of experience from which to draw when working with social services users. Understandably, younger staff in management, social work and residential work were less likely to have had such experience prior to entry to work. Data comparing the average ages of staff in the statutory, voluntary and private sectors has shown that, in the 1990s, staff in residential and home care in the voluntary and private care sectors are, on average, younger than in the statutory workforce (LGMB, 1997b). Given the growth of the voluntary and private sectors, increasing the numbers of younger staff could have implications for the quality of service provided in work which particularly demands the kind of sensitivity to and awareness of others' needs gained through experience. There are also implications for the type of training required.

The work histories revealed that younger staff had a higher rate of job turnover. This was true for all job types and for both women and men, though in residential and home care work men changed jobs twice as often as women. While job turnover has its benefits for those who are mobile, it is much less appreciated by service users, who value continuity of care from people who have become familiar with their needs (Harding and Beresford, 1996). It also poses major problems for employers in recruitment costs and time. Again there is evidence of higher turnover levels in the growing private sector of residential and home care and there is justifiable concern that this could undermine the quality of service delivery (LGMB, 1997b).

The career patterns within social services over the last 30 years have often deviated from the conventional progression through an unbroken period of service, and have shown staff leaving and rejoining social services in surprising numbers. After their first job in social services for example, at least a quarter of staff had left and then rejoined, and a third had done this more than once. This was particularly noticeable among older staff in management and social work and among younger residential workers. Many of the reasons for leaving were associated with training or leaving to have a family, but clearly others had moved to different types of work and then returned. We can only speculate at this stage as to the possible implications of this. On the positive side it indicates both flexibility and commitment, with job content and life experiences, rather than career aspirations, possibly proving the dominant force. On the negative side, this pattern defies professional training approaches and career advancement and may well mean that some, particularly women, do not achieve their full potential in a senior position.

There are indications in this chapter of some of the changes that have taken place in social work training. In all three samples, social workers in the 1990s were found to be more likely than previously to undertake qualifying training before their first social services job, rather than after they had joined social services. Younger and less experienced students come into training with a different knowledge base from that of mature students, and while, having left school more recently, their study skills may be superior, they will usually have less experience of those issues central to social work and social care. However, Marsh and Triseliotis found that 60% of the intake to non-graduate social work courses had over five years of social services experience prior to training, so this development may only relate to graduates (Marsh and Triseliotis, 1996).

The majority of staff reported having dependent children living with them at some time during their working lives. The Workforce studies also established that about a quarter of the workforce were caring for dependent adults and that only about a fifth of women social work staff who had a baby after joining social services took maternity leave. Given these two findings, there is a clear need in social services for family friendly employment policies.

Family friendly policies are of particular significance in local labour markets. Data from the work histories reflects the local labour markets within which much of the workforce operates. In England nearly half of managers and social work staff (43%) had previously been employed by two or three other authorities in addition to the one in which they were employed when the survey took place, but only 2% of home care workers and 11% of residential workers had ever worked for another authority. Most home care workers and residential workers are women, who often work close to home because of their caring responsibilities. This means that competition for their relatively low paid labour is local from, for example, supermarkets and small factories. Employers increasingly faced with staff shortages need to recognise the strength of local competition and create workplace conditions which will attract staff and encourage them to stay in post.

A workforce with discontinuous career patterns and with substantial family commitments is one which social services employers will need to work hard to retain. This is reinforced by the current climate encouraging movement between the statutory, voluntary and private sectors. Historically this has been minimal and provides no precedence for the growth of staff numbers now taking place in the voluntary and private sectors. The study suggests a reluctance by statutory staff to make such a transition, and the danger is that their skills and qualifications will not be available to other employers if workplace conditions in voluntary and private care sectors are not at least comparable to those experienced by staff in the statutory sector.

THREE

The changing nature of work

Susan Balloch and John McLean

Moving from the work histories to present working conditions, this chapter illustrates the typical conditions of employment and the responsibilities and activities carried out by staff, and looks at how staff thought their work had changed between first and second interviews. It is structured around the four job types of manager, field social work staff, home care worker and residential worker, and is based on responses from those who were interviewed twice. These included 940 staff from five local authority social services departments in England, 317 staff from two social work departments in Scotland and 320 staff from the four Health and Social Service Boards and their Trusts in Northern Ireland (see Chapter One). We will show the high degree of consistency among staff in the three studies in their experiences of work and in their priorities in practice. We will also show how structural and legislative changes in welfare have created additional administrative work and reduced the time spent in direct contact with users.

Service user groups

A majority of staff in each study said their work focused on a particular group of service users, a majority with one main group but many with more than one group. Field social work staff were most likely to be working with children and families, whereas residential workers more commonly worked with older people, and home care workers almost exclusively so. There were a number of gender similarities across the three studies, with women more likely to be working with older people, even in management, and male residential workers more likely to be working with young people and users with learning difficulties or mental health problems. In Scotland a higher percentage of men in field social work were involved in criminal justice work than women (24% to 3%).

In England just 2% of staff worked specifically with an ethnic minority group (first interview finding). This pattern represents a continuation of previous involvement of men in specific areas, particularly with adolescents, criminal justice and mental health. Very few men worked in home care, and none at all were found in the Northern Ireland study. Most men in home care were employed in the inner London authority, which, as mentioned previously, had a policy of employing home care workers on full-time contracts. Once again this emphasises men's association with full-time work. These findings indicate the persistence of traditional working patterns, built up over the last 50 years as the personal social services have taken shape. They will surely be subject to review as new approaches to children's and adults' services are developed.

Hours of work

Defining full-time work as 30 hours a week or more, we found that nearly all men in the social services worked full-time at both first and second interviews, but about half of all women worked part-time. In England, for example, only 10% of men worked part-time compared with 50% of women, including 63% of women with a child under 12; in Scotland only 4% of men compared with 51% of women worked part-time; in Northern Ireland no men at all worked part-time, but 11% of women managers, field social work staff and residential staff did so, as did 93% of home care staff.

As the Northern Ireland figures indicate, each of the four job types exhibited a different pattern of full- and part-time work. Almost all managers worked full-time, as did between 80% and 90% of field social work staff. Full-time working was, however, uncommon among home care staff except in one English social services department which had a specific policy to employ these staff full-time. The widest variation between the three study areas was found among residential workers: in England 37% worked part-time, compared with only 12% in Scotland and 8% in Northern Ireland. The Northern Ireland figure was influenced by the selection of mainly residential workers mainly in childcare, who were more likely to work full-time. Gender differences in hours worked existed within all the job types, but, as shown in Table 3.1, were most pronounced among home care staff.

Table 3.1: Percentages of women and men working part-time in each job type at second interview

Staff working part-time		Managers	Field social work staff	Home care workers	Residential workers
England					
	Women	5	19	76	35
	Men	2	8	23	14
Scotland					
	Women	17	13	79	14
	Men	2	2	0	2
Northern Ireland					
	Women	7	18	9	93
	Men	–	–	–	–

The extent of part-time working is important because it has been associated with restricted career development, which is discussed in detail in Chapter Eight.

Those interviewed were also asked if they worked beyond their official hours and, if so, whether or not this work was paid or unpaid. A proportion of staff in each job type worked overtime but this was most likely for managers and field social work staff (Table 3.2). Home care workers in Scotland appeared to be the least likely to work beyond their hours.

Table 3.2: Percentages of staff who worked more than their official hours

Staff working more than their official hours	Managers	Field social work staff	Home care workers	Residential workers
England	78	66	54	45
Scotland	84	73	13	35
Northern Ireland	75	70	39	49

Across the three studies the picture was one of substantial overtime worked by managers and field social work staff, particularly men managers, most of which was unpaid. Overtime worked by home care and residential workers was much more likely to be paid. In England overtime working had increased between interviews from an average of 3.2 to 3.7 hours extra per week, a finding consistent with reports by staff of having to spend more time carrying out core tasks. At the same time, the overall gender difference in overtime working had narrowed: at first interview 52% of women and 70% of men said they worked overtime compared with 57% of women and 65% of men at the second interview. However, at second interview there was still a significant gender difference among managers, with 74% of women compared with 85% of men working overtime.

The European Union's Working Time Directive (WTD) seeks to limit most employees' average hours to 48 per week (TUC, 1996). In the economy as a whole, 6% of non-manual men and less than 2% of manual women worked over 48 hours per week (LGMB, 1996). At second interview, a minority of social services staff in England usually worked over 48 hours. Most of these worked with adolescents or people with mental health problems in a residential setting or day centre. Clearly employing authorities will need to review policies on overtime to comply with the WTD, particularly in residential work where there are implications for the amount of time staff have off between late and early shifts and for sleeping in duties.

Take home pay

Taking full-time staff at first interview, the majority of managers and field social work staff in all three studies, and residential workers in Northern Ireland, took home over £800 per month, the Northern Ireland figure partly reflecting the higher proportion of residential childcare workers in that study. Other staff, those who provided direct care for users – home care workers and residential workers – took home less. Table 3.3, based on the first interviews in England, illustrates the pattern common to all three studies of men earning more than women in full-time work in each job type. These findings were compatible with those of the British Household Panel Survey (BHPS) (Buck et al, 1994), though more managers in our study took home over £1,200 per month.

Table 3.3: Take home pay of full-time workers at first interview in England: percentages by job type and gender

Take home pay per month	Managers		Field social work staff		Home care workers		Residential workers	
	W	M	W	M	W	M	W	M
Less than £400	<1	<1	0	1	18	0	4	2
£400 to £800	4	2	17	5	74	84	63	41
£800 to £1,199	46	24	56	52	8	13	26	46
More than £1,200	48	71	27	41	3	0	9	40

W = women   M = men

In the second interview, instead of asking respondents to place themselves within the broad pay bands above, we recorded the exact amount of take home pay and this allowed us to calculate hourly net pay based on all hours including overtime. In England, for staff as a whole, the mean net hourly pay was £5.40. Women's hourly pay was on average nearly £2 less than men's. One reason for this was occupational (or horizontal) gender segregation, exemplified by the higher proportion of women working in home care where pay rates were lowest. For 27 home care workers, their net hourly pay was £3 or less, indicating that their gross pay was probably under £4 per hour. Within each job type, except for home care where the difference was slight, there was a significant gap between women's and men's net hourly pay: the ratio of women's pay to men's was 0.86 for managers, 0.92 for social work staff and 0.88 for residential workers. Although these figures may have been affected by differences between the authorities such as the higher proportion of women in a metropolitan borough in an area of generally depressed wages, and staff in the London authorities receiving either London Weighting or London Allowance, the differences suggest a degree of vertical segregation by gender, with women more likely to be employed in the lower grades of each occupation and at lower management levels than men (Ginn, 1997).

These findings should be viewed in the context of the discussion in Chapter Six of equal opportunities policies and the occupational attainment of women and men discussed in Chapter Seven.

Responsibilities of each job type

The second interview provided an opportunity to ask workers about their responsibilities, and about the activities and tasks on which they spent their time. We will review the findings for each job type, illustrating the similarities and differences between the three studies.

Managers

Staff were asked to name all the responsibilities held by them from a comprehensive list and to identify which three were the most important. Managers' main responsibilities are shown in Table 3.4, arbitrarily listed in order of the responses in England. The three most frequently cited, which are shaded, did not necessarily coincide with the level of importance. For example, although 'managing a budget' was the sixth most often mentioned by English managers, it was third most likely to be listed as one of the most important parts of the job.

Table 3.4: Main responsibilities of managers

Type of task	England		Scotland		Northern Ireland	
	%	Importance	%	Importance	%	Importance
Staff supervision	93	I	92	I	98	2
Recruitment	81		65		83	
Managing a service	81	2	74	2	94	I
Training others	75		83		73	
Planning	75		78	3	86	3
Managing a budget	73	3	67		66	
Quality assurance	70		64		76	
Joint working	66		62		75	
Service provision	66		61		77	
Case conferences	58		72		78	
sample n	**276**		**87**		**76**	

There was a considerable degree of agreement. In Scotland and Northern Ireland, the three most important parts of the job were identified as managing a service, staff supervision and planning. In England the most important were staff supervision, managing a service and managing a budget. On balance, across the three workforces this represents a broadly similar view of the management task and its priorities.

Evidence emerged of different duties and priorities for women and men managers. In England men were more likely than women to have worked on policy development (73% compared with 49%), with elected members (24% versus 10%), and in criminal justice (14% versus 2%). In Northern Ireland the proportion of men identifying policy development was almost twice that of women (73% and 39%), and men were also more likely to list planning, commissioning and managing a budget among their activities. In both England and Northern Ireland women were more likely to do counselling and, in Northern Ireland, to attend case conferences and reviews. Although gender differences were generally not as great as in the other studies, in Scotland it was women who were more often involved in policy development and managing a service, whereas men more often mentioned service provision, care management and quality assurance. Three quarters of managers in England also included equal opportunities among their main activities, but this was identified by only 1% in Scotland.

Staff were asked which tasks and activities formed part of their work, which occupied the greatest amount of time in the last week, and if they were spending more or less time on each compared with the first interview. Table 3.5 shows the activities carried out by managers. The percentage column gives the proportion in each study who referred to this activity, with the six most frequently mentioned shaded. The second column for each study gives the three activities which occupied the greatest amount of time in the last week.

The same six activities were most often mentioned by managers in each study: attending meetings, telephoning, supervision, report writing, filling in forms/record keeping and attending case conferences and reviews. There was a degree of congruence across the three studies for every activity on the list, suggesting that social services managers in England and Northern Ireland have a common, clearly defined role. The same three activities occupied the greatest amount of time in the last week, albeit in a different order in each study; meetings, supervision and face to face contact with users. In England and Northern Ireland, the activity mentioned by the highest proportion was attending meetings, in Scotland it was supervision.

Table 3.5: Managers' activities: most often mentioned and most time last week

	England		Scotland		Northern Ireland	
Activity	%	Most time last week	%	Most time last week	%	Most time last week
Meetings	96	1	96	2	96	1
Telephoning	93		96		99	
Supervising/being supervised	91	3	92	1	95	2
Report writing	89		88		88	
Filling in forms/ record keeping	82		86		85	
Case conferences/ reviews	76		90		84	
Face-to-face contact	72	2	83	3	75	3
Travelling at work	71		81		79	
Training	69		80		73	
Assessment	60		79		80	
Counselling other staff	57		62		65	
Court attendance	18		13		24	
Other	59		53		52	

Managers reported that time spent on several aspects of the work, mainly administrative tasks and procedures, had increased. Compared with the first interview, two thirds in England and half in Scotland and Northern Ireland were spending more time writing reports, filling in forms, record keeping, attending meetings and telephoning. Not all extra time was expended on bureaucracy however, with similar proportions reporting increases in time spent on staff supervision, and 40% more time on training. Fewer managers reported spending less time on any particular activities, the main reductions being half in England and Scotland and a third in Northern Ireland spending less time in face-to-face contact with users, and a quarter in England and Scotland spending less time travelling on work-related business.

Staff were asked about the extent to which recent changes had affected the section or unit in which they worked. There was general agreement among managers in the three studies, with two thirds saying that restructuring, the introduction of the community care legislation and cuts in funding had affected their section or unit 'a great deal' or 'quite a lot'. Some changes had particularly affected specific categories of staff, especially managers in Scotland, two thirds of whom said their section had been affected by local government reorganisation (with the replacement of regions by smaller unitary authorities, see Chapter One), and in Northern Ireland, where three quarters had been affected by health service and general management reforms (reorganisation of the four Health and Social Services Boards into Trusts, again see Chapter One). Other changes had varying effects on the sections or units of managers in each study, but the privatisation and contracting out of services, specialisation and decreased in-house provision affected approximately a third. Smaller proportions, a quarter in England, cited the introduction of the 1989 Children Act (or the equivalent 1995 Children [Scotland] Act, 16%); the 1995 Children (Northern Ireland) Order, 44%; relocation, charging policies or increased in-house provision.

Apart from the effect on the section or unit in which they worked, recent changes also had an impact on the ability of staff to carry out their own work. The main consequence of change for managers was different demands being made of them: this affected four out of five in England and Northern Ireland and two thirds in Scotland. Approximately two thirds said that change had resulted in them having to learn new skills, a third said that it had brought about reductions in staffing, had created greater job insecurity, retraining and increases in user complaints. Smaller proportions said that change had also resulted in the introduction of team working, colleagues leaving for jobs elsewhere and redundancies. Very few staff had been affected by other consequences of change such as increased paid overtime or fewer users taking up services, and change had produced little in the way of benefits for staff, with for example, more opportunities for promotion.

Field social work staff

Table 3.6 shows the responsibilities of field social work staff with the three most often cited in each study shaded.

As with managers, there was a high level of consistency in the three studies in terms of the most frequently mentioned. In Scotland and Northern Ireland, family support was the most important part of the job; in England the most important were care management, with duty social work second, followed by family support. The second and third most important parts of the job in Scotland were child protection and counselling, and in Northern Ireland, counselling and service provision.

Table 3.6: Main responsibilities of field social work staff

Type of task	England %	Importance	Scotland %	Importance	Northern Ireland %	Importance
Case conferences	77		74		79	
Counselling	75		86	3	89	2
Joint working	69		63		53	
Duty social work	66	2	59		55	
Family support	62	3	67	1	70	1
Advocacy	57		56		63	
Care management	56	1	43		45	
Service provision	53		55		58	3
Hospital discharge	47		?		40	
Child protection	45		49	2	52	
Welfare rights	45		67		50	
Training	36		43		40	
sample n	216		79		121	

Activities carried out by field social work staff are shown in Table 3.7, with the six most frequently mentioned shaded.

Although slightly more diverse than the main activities of managers, field social work staff in each study referred to a common core of similar or related tasks. Thus, most were involved in report writing, filling in forms and record keeping, telephoning, face-to-face contact with users and assessment, and, as with managers, on all activities listed similarities with colleagues elsewhere were more pronounced than differences. In each study face-to-face contact with users occupied the greatest amount of time in the last week; the other most time-consuming activities were report writing, filling in forms in England, and assessment in Scotland and Northern Ireland.

As with managers, field social work staff also said they were spending more time on administrative procedures, particularly filling in forms and record keeping, which applied to 79% in England, half in Scotland, and two thirds in Northern Ireland. This is consistent with the findings of other studies, in particular Levin and Webb (1997). Time spent on report writing and telephoning had increased in all three studies; time in meetings, assessment and travelling had increased for staff in Scotland and Northern Ireland. However, there was less congruence over other activities. A third in England and Northern Ireland were spending less time on face-to-face contact with users, while another third in England, and a quarter in Northern Ireland and Scotland spent more time on this. In addition, a third in England spent less time on training, whereas two fifths in Scotland and Northern Ireland spent more time training.

Table 3.7 Field social work staff's activities: most often mentioned and most time last week

Activity	England %	Most time last week	Scotland %	Most time last week	Northern Ireland %	Most time last week
Filling in forms/ record keeping	94	2	89		95	
Meetings	93		84		97	
Telephoning	93		92		99	
Report writing	91	3	91	3	96	2
Face-to-face contact	91	1	84	1	97	1
Assessment	89		88	2	93	3
Travelling at work	88		90		93	
Case conferences/ reviews	86		86		93	
Being trained	66		58		70	
Court attendance	44		38		39	
Supervising/being supervised	42		47		62	
Counselling other staff	42		18		27	
Other	54		49		48	

Field social work staff reported that their sections or units were affected by the same recent changes as managers: three quarters by cuts in funding, two thirds by the Community Care legislation and restructuring. Two thirds in Scotland were affected by local government reorganisation and a similar proportion in Northern Ireland by reorganisation of the four Health and Social Services Boards into Trusts. Half in each study were affected by Health Service reforms, and half in England and Northern Ireland were affected by the Children Act/Order. Higher proportions in

England mentioned the effects of privatisation and contracting out of services, specialisation, decreased in-house provision, and approximately a quarter in each study were affected by relocation and new charging policies or increased in-house provision.

Change also affected field social work staff's ability to carry out their own work. As with managers, this was most often caused by different demands being made, particularly in England; the need to learn new skills; reduced staffing, again particularly in England; greater job insecurity especially in Scotland, and in England and Scotland, people leaving for jobs elsewhere and redundancies.

Home care workers

Home care workers' main responsibilities are shown in Table 3.8, the three most frequently mentioned in each study including preparing meals, domestic work and shopping. However, there were interesting differences between staff in England and those in Scotland and Northern Ireland. In England, 94% of home care staff were providing personal care; in Scotland 69% were doing this and in Northern Ireland, personal care was only mentioned by 39%. Giving emotional support was more often mentioned by English and Scottish staff than by those in Northern Ireland (three quarters compared with half), as was giving medication, which involved half of home care workers in England and Scotland, but just over a third in Northern Ireland. Personal care was the most important part of the job in England, followed by preparing meals and providing social and emotional support. Preparation of meals was considered to be the most important part of the job in Scotland, with shopping second and personal care third; domestic work, preparing meals and shopping were the most important in Northern Ireland. These findings are consistent with those referred to below, which show that more home care workers in England than in the other studies were affected by the community care legislation.

Table 3.9 shows the activities carried out by home care workers, with the three most frequently mentioned shaded.

Table 3.8: Main responsibilities of home care workers

Type of task	England %	Importance	Scotland %	Importance	Northern Ireland %	Importance
Personal care	94	I	69	3	39	
Preparing meals	93	2	97	I	87	2
Domestic work	83		94		96	I
Shopping	82		96	2	93	3
Collecting pensions/ benefits	81		91		74	
Social and emotional support	79	3	72		54	
Giving medication	51		50		39	
Counselling	17		5		8	
Develop care programmes	7		3		0	
Parenting	3		I		0	
Staff supervision	2		0		0	
sample n	248		82		54	

Table 3.9: Home care workers' activities: most often mentioned and most time last week

Activity	England %	Most time last week	Scotland %	Most time last week	Northern Ireland %	Most time last week
Face-to-face contact	98	I	98	I	100	I
Meetings	78	3	24		14	
Filling in forms/ record keeping	56		30		31	
Telephoning	55		51		38	
Training	40		14		2	
Assessment	38		38		5	
Travelling at work	37	2	47		5	
Case conferences/ reviews	25		6		0	
Report writing	22		4		0	
Supervising/being supervised	7		2		0	
Other	16		9		14	

As might be expected, face-to-face contact with users was the activity mentioned most often by home care workers. There were variations between the studies in how often other activities were mentioned. In England attending meetings was the second most often referred to, followed by filling in forms; in Scotland and Northern Ireland second and third included, telephoning, travelling and filling in forms. Face-to-face contact occupied the greatest amount of time in the last week, in England travelling the second greatest, but very few staff in Scotland and Northern Ireland mentioned other particularly time-consuming activities.

There were fewer changes in the activities of home care workers than there had been for the other job types. Two fifths of home care workers in England spent increased time in face-to-face contact with users, a fifth more time filling in forms, record keeping, telephoning and assessment. In Scotland a fifth spent more time travelling between users' homes, and whereas a small number of English staff said they were spending less time on training, in Scotland, as with field social work staff, a sixth spent more time on this. Time spent on different activities by home care workers in Northern Ireland had changed very little.

On the whole, fewer home care workers than other job types said that recent changes had affected their section or unit. The main sources had been the community care legislation and cuts in funding, which had affected half of staff in England and a third in Scotland, but less than a fifth in Northern Ireland. In England and Scotland, the units or sections of between a fifth and a third of staff had been affected by privatisation, contracting out, restructuring, local government reorganisation, Health Service reforms, new charging policies and decreased in-house provision. However, very few home care workers in Northern Ireland felt that recent changes had affected their section or unit a lot.

The effect of changes on home care workers' ability to carry out their work varied considerably between the studies. In England, almost half felt that different demands were being made, in Scotland a third felt this. In England a quarter were affected by the need to learn new skills, reduced staffing, greater job insecurity, a fifth by the introduction of team working, fewer users taking up services and reduced hours of work. A third of Scottish home care workers had to learn new skills, a quarter undertake retraining and a fifth felt there was greater job insecurity and reduced staffing. Very few home care workers in Northern Ireland were affected by any changes, for example, only 17% by reduced hours, 11% by greater job insecurity.

Residential workers

The responsibilities of residential workers are shown in Table 3.10, again with the three most often mentioned shaded. The three most important parts of the job were broadly the same as the three most often cited, which, in all three studies included providing social and emotional support. The other most important parts of the job were: in England and Scotland, providing personal care; in England and Northern Ireland, giving medication; and in Scotland and Northern Ireland, developing and implementing care programmes. These proportions reflect not only the diversity of responsibilities carried out, but also the differences between staff who were residential workers with children, and staff who were care assistants with older people.

Table 3.10: Main responsibilities of residential workers

	England		Scotland		Northern Ireland	
Type of task	%	Importance	%	Importance	%	Importance
Personal care	84	I	83	2	75	3
Social/ emotional support	83	2	95	I	96	I
Giving medication	71	3	75		90	
Preparing meals	67		58		52	
Domestic work	63		52		45	
Shopping	63		54		63	
Develop care programmes	60		83	3	91	2
Counselling	41		59		72	
Staff supervision	20		39		55	
Parenting	17		20		35	
Collecting pensions	12		25		27	
Other	13		19		22	
sample n	**200**		**69**		**69**	

The activities carried out by residential workers most often are shown in Table 3.11, with the five most frequently mentioned shaded, and the three which occupied the greatest amount of time in the last week in the second column.

Table 3.11: Residential workers' activities: most often mentioned and most time last week

Activity	England %	Most time last week	Scotland %	Most time last week	Northern Ireland %	Most time last week
Face-to-face contact	97	1	90	1	97	
Report writing	90	2	95	3	100	2
Filling in forms/ record keeping	81		89	2	100	1
Meetings	80		79		99	
Assessment	72	3	89		82	3
Being trained	65		56		74	
Telephoning	61		78		100	
Case conferences/ reviews	61		58		97	
Travelling at work	47		61		75	
Supervising/being supervised	36		41		78	
Counselling other staff	19		25		31	
Court attendance	9		24		33	
Other	48		37		68	

As with the other job types, residential workers in the three studies had a great deal in common in terms of the activities which occupied them at work. Broadly the same tasks were mentioned most often: face-to-face contact with users; filling in forms and record keeping; report writing; meetings; and assessment, and these were generally felt to be the most time-consuming in the last week.

Between half and two thirds of residential workers were spending increased time on writing reports, record keeping, filling in forms, carrying out assessments and training; in Scotland and Northern Ireland a third spent more time telephoning, in meetings and in face-to-face contact with users.

Cuts in funding had affected the section or unit of half of residential workers in England and Northern Ireland, and a quarter in Scotland. Across the studies, between one and two fifths were affected by restructuring, the community care legislation, local government reorganisation and Health Service reforms. In Northern Ireland half had been affected by the reorgansiation of Boards into Trusts, and a third by privatisation and contracting out of services.

Apart from the effect on the section or unit in which they worked, recent changes also had an impact on residential workers' ability to carry out their own work. Two thirds in England and Northern Ireland had been affected by different demands being made of them, and half in Scotland. Reduced staffing and the need to learn new skills affected half in Northern Ireland and a third in England and Scotland, and between a fifth and a third across the studies were affected by greater job insecurity, introduction of team working, retraining and people leaving for jobs elsewhere.

For a third of each job type, change had also created greater job insecurity, which was particularly felt in Scotland, by almost half of field social work staff. However, it has to be noted that, in contrast, only 11% of home care workers in Northern Ireland and the same proportion of residential workers in Scotland thought their jobs were less secure. Between a quarter and a third of staff were affected by other aspects of change, including increases in user complaints; retraining; introduction of team working; and particularly affecting field social work staff, colleagues leaving for jobs elsewhere. Relatively few staff had been affected by other consequences of change such as redundancies, increased paid overtime or fewer users taking up services, and change had produced little in the way of benefits for staff, for example, more opportunities for promotion.

Conclusions

By focusing on the four selected job types of manager, field social work staff, home care worker and residential worker this chapter provides an essential background to the rest of the book. The job types are quite distinct from one another, the responsibilities and activities carried out by each are quite different, and it is important to bear these differences in mind in the discussion of other aspects of work experience. As in Chapter Two, we have identified a division between office based staff in management and field social work, and staff who provide direct care for service users, that is, home care and residential workers. The differences were evident in nearly all aspects of the job, including the gender of the workers, hours of work, pay, user groups, responsibilities and tasks carried out. However, there was also evidence of similarities within each job type across the three studies, with consistency in the reporting of responsibilities, job activities and the amount of time spent on different tasks, regardless of whether staff worked in England, Scotland or Northern Ireland. In view of the difficulties encountered in defining roles within social services (NISW, 1982; Davies, 1985), these similarities must be considered to be a major strength, with very positive implications for setting and maintaining standards of care, providing training, recognising existing qualifications and establishing new ones. Such similarities should also facilitate staff mobility, making it easier for employers to recruit new managers and other staff with appropriate experience, and facilitating the introduction and development of new initiatives and sharing of ideas and knowledge between different employers.

Staff in each job type identified similar aspects of work that were placing greater demands on them. Many of these were the results of recent legislation and restructuring of departments and Boards, and convey a certain amount of frustration by staff over what was perceived to be increasing paperwork and bureaucracy. In the two year period covered by the studies, staff in all four job types reported increases in the time spent on broadly similar activities, particularly paperwork, which was one of the greatest sources of dissatisfaction (Chapter Four; see also Levin and Webb, 1997). The issue of increased paperwork and other forms of bureaucracy is also discussed in Chapter Nine in the context of reasons given by staff for changing jobs. This is particularly relevant to one of the main themes addressed by this book, that the social services workforce is stable, committed and resilient, but is not indestructible and cannot necessarily withstand constant change. Many of the consequences of recent changes are revisited in later chapters, particularly in the discussions of satisfaction, stress, training, career progression and staff who change jobs.

FOUR

Satisfaction, stress and control over work

John McLean

In Chapter Three we described the range of different activities carried out by social services staff in the course of their work. In this chapter we will consider staff's experience of carrying out this work. Allowing for related activities such as travel, full-time employees might spend a third or more of their lives at work. In view of this, it would be reasonable for workers to expect their work to be rewarding and worthwhile, not just as a source of income, but as a source of fulfilment from which they can feel that their time and effort have been usefully spent. It is also reasonable for workers to expect their work to be stimulating without subjecting them to unreasonable frustration or stress. Although not everyone will have a job that provides this, failure to address lack of job satisfaction and stress can affect staff performance, morale and commitment, which in turn will affect the functioning and productivity of the organisation (Landy, 1989).

Social services are dependent on achieving the best performance from their staff. It might be argued that, as with nursing or teaching, jobs in social services caring for others rely more heavily on personal commitment, often for lower pay than staff might earn in other occupations. It can be very rewarding contributing to the lives of some of the most disadvantaged people. It can also be very stressful working with people who may be demanding and uncooperative, or acting as law enforcers in work with children or people with mental health problems. Social services departments and Boards are generally aware of the pressures on their staff, and provide extensive supervision and training programmes, a fact confirmed by the account of training in Chapter Eight.

We will look at satisfaction and stress and how other aspects of work experience are related to these, particularly control, role conflict and sickness absence. The work carried out by managers, field social work staff, home care and residential workers differs considerably, and it might be expected that staff in each job type will experience satisfaction and stress differently. Tasks carried out have been described in Chapter Three in relation to the changing nature of the work, and in previous Workforce reports (Balloch et al, 1995; McConkey et al, 1997; Buglass et al, 1998), but to summarise briefly, managers are involved in administration, planning, decision making, employment and supervision of staff, and have little contact with service users. Most are women, but there is a higher proportion of men than in the other job types, particularly at higher levels (see also Chapter Seven).

Field social work staff are office-based and are mainly responsible for caseload management, assessing needs, organising services, administration, statutory duties and liaising with other service providers. Typically, they spend up to a third of their time in direct contact with users (Fein and Staff, 1991; Levin and Webb, 1997), their work often requires a counselling approach and involves difficult decision making about priority, risk or even culpability. Field social work staff are mostly women, but it is the second most common job type for men.

Home care workers usually work on their own and spend most of their time in users' homes. Mostly part-time, they use the office as a base, and have little contact with colleagues or managers. Most are women and are involved in preparing meals, shopping and providing personal care. Central to being able to carry out the work is cooperation based on the quality of relationship with users (Bartoldus et al, 1989; Warren, 1990).

Residential workers provide direct care for users who live in care. About a third are part-time, and this is the only job type for which shift work, including night duty and sleeping in, is the norm. They work with colleagues as part of a team, and the residential home is often perceived as the workplace rather than the employing authority. Most residential workers are women, although there is a higher proportion of men in childcare.

Satisfaction

A quality service requires committed staff who obtain satisfaction from their work. Research has shown that satisfaction often differs according to occupational level, and varies between different groups. Usually only a minority of workers express dissatisfaction. Satisfaction is more often attributed to factors associated with individual effort, accomplishment, achievement, recognition, responsibility, advancement and salary.

Dissatisfaction is more often attributed to something or someone other than the individual, such as the supervisor, other workers, the administration, technical supervision, working conditions or company policy (Hertzberg et al, 1957). Different elements of satisfaction are important to different individuals (Locke, 1976). Thus if a high salary is important to someone, and relationships with colleagues are not, this person will be dissatisfied if the pay is low, no matter how pleasant their colleagues. Warr (1987) concluded that individuals are just as likely to vary in the satisfaction they obtain from different work tasks as they are from different sources of satisfaction in other areas of life.

In the Workforce studies, there was a very high level of concordance within each of the four job types as to the most satisfying aspects of the job.

Managers and field social work staff

The most satisfying aspects of the work, for over three quarters of managers and field social work staff, were associated with their own individual efforts:

- the freedom to choose their own working methods;
- making progress in difficult work;
- feeling they had helped people;
- their fellow workers;
- being part of a team that works well together;
- the variety and challenge of the work;
- the amount of responsibility.

Two thirds gained satisfaction from opportunities to use their abilities and ideas, sharing skills, working creatively and the quality of service they were personally able to provide. Similar proportions were satisfied with the hours of work, job security, the work environment, their immediate boss and the amount of control they had.

However, only half were satisfied with aspects of the work not attributable to their own efforts, particularly gratitude from users, recognition for good work, pay, relationships between management and staff, scope for self-development and the quality of the service generally. Only a third were satisfied with:

- chances of promotion;
- the amount of influence they had if they thought something needed to be changed;
- the number of deadlines;

- attention paid to suggestions;
- the way the department is managed;
- the amount of time they could devote to in-depth work.

The least satisfying aspect of all, for only 10%, were the volume of paperwork and the amount of change going on, a direct reflection of the perceived changes in these aspects of the work reported in Chapter Three.

Most of the differences between managers and field social work staff reflected the job content. Managers were more satisfied with the scope for trying out ideas and for self-development, relationships between management and staff and the quality of the service generally. Making progress in a difficult case, gratitude from users, and job security were more satisfying for field social work staff.

In general, there was greater satisfaction among managers and field social work staff in Northern Ireland and Scotland on most items than in England. In Northern Ireland this was particularly the case for satisfaction with the immediate boss, opportunities to use abilities and recognition for good work.

Home care workers and residential workers

Tasks which produced rewards in response to their own efforts were also the most satisfying for home care and residential workers. Most of these were associated with aspects of the relationship with users: up to 90% obtained satisfaction from keeping users clean and comfortable, seeing them make progress, being confided in and being missed when they were off duty. Over three quarters were satisfied with:

- the quality of service they personally were able to give;
- the amount of responsibility;
- the way the team works together;
- relationships with health professionals;
- the quality of service generally;
- amount of control they had over what they had to do.

In addition, most were satisfied with the working environment, including fellow workers, the immediate boss, relationships between management and staff, the hours of work and physical working conditions.

An important element of satisfaction is feedback (Landy, 1989), and between half and two thirds felt satisfied with recognition for good work and the attention paid to their suggestions. Perhaps reflecting the nature of the job, over half were satisfied with the amount of paperwork, the number of deadlines, job security and the way the department was managed. However, the implication is that up to half were not satisfied with these.

The least satisfying were the amount of influence they had if they thought something needed to be changed, their chances of promotion, the amount of time they could devote to in-depth work and the amount of change taking place, all aspects outside of their control, all attributable to somebody else.

Home care workers obtained greater satisfaction than staff in the other three job types from nearly all aspects of the work. This was perhaps a consequence of working alone much of the time, resulting in greater sense of control over what they do. Thus, very high satisfaction was derived from the freedom to choose their own working methods, the variety of tasks and the opportunity to use their abilities. In contrast, staff in the other three job types were more often affected by other people in the organisation and job conditions.

Some differences between job types were very pronounced. To give two examples, in Northern Ireland two thirds of residential workers were satisfied with the amount of influence they had, whereas only a third of home care workers were, and in Scotland, 87% of home care workers were satisfied with the amount of paperwork, compared with only 9% of Scottish managers.

For most staff then, regardless of the job type, the greatest satisfaction came from aspects over which they had the greatest control, which produced rewards attributable to their own efforts. Least satisfying were aspects over which they had least control which were attributable to somebody or something else. Most staff responded positively to most items, but on every item some staff, often up to half, were not satisfied. This has to be considered in the context of other research which has suggested that only a minority of workers express dissatisfaction (Landy, 1989).

The amount of change taking place was a common factor in the level of dissatisfaction in each of the three studies. This was not confined to Scotland and Northern Ireland, where disruption might have been expected during preparations for the reorganisation of Northern Ireland Boards into Trusts, and Scottish Regions into smaller unitary authorities. Change in England was also a cause of dissatisfaction, even though local authority reorganisation had not yet been implemented, suggesting that as was reported in Chapter Three, staff were affected by specialisation of services, the introduction of the purchaser–provider split and other changes in response to the 1989 Children Act and the 1990 National Health Service and Community Care Act. Change is inevitable if organisations are to adapt and evolve, but these findings emphasise the need to involve staff in the process to enable them to retain control, and to minimise disruption (see also Smale, 1996).

Measuring satisfaction

To enable us to identify staff who are satisfied, and more importantly, staff who are dissatisfied, it is necessary to measure satisfaction to allow examination of associated factors. In the Workforce studies we used a set of 15 statements devised by Warr et al (1979) which measure intrinsic and extrinsic job satisfaction. Responses to each statement were scored to give a maximum of 105, and the mean scores for different categories were calculated, the higher the score, the greater the satisfaction. To give a context to the results in the Workforce studies, the mean score in a study of men blue collar workers was 69.86, and in a study of women and men university graduates it was 74.61 (Warr et al, 1979). Table 4.1 gives the mean satisfaction scores for the three samples at the first and second interviews.

Table 4.1: Mean satisfaction scores at first and second interviews

	Mean satisfaction scores	
	First interview	Second interview
England	71.03	69.74
Scotland	71.89	73.42
Northern Ireland	70.03	72.07

Mean scores were comparable with those in the study by Warr et al. By the second interview there had been moderate increases for staff in Northern Ireland and Scotland, whereas in England satisfaction had declined slightly. At both interviews, mean scores were lower for men, staff aged less than 40, staff in manager, field social work and residential jobs, and those working with children and families. Conversely, satisfaction was higher among women, staff over 50 years, home care workers and those who worked with older people.

Satisfaction levels differed between other categories of staff, for example, in England, black staff had lower scores than white staff, and in Northern

Ireland, Catholic staff had lower scores than Protestant staff. In England the mean scores at the second interview ranged from 60.47 for the (largely dissatisfied) staff in the inner London authority, to 72.63 for home care workers. In Northern Ireland, scores ranged from 64.92 for staff in one Board at the first interview, to 75.92 for home care workers at the second interview; and in Scotland at the second interview they ranged from 63.17 for men, to 79.89 for staff aged 50 or over.

Mean scores for satisfaction will be used later in this chapter to examine the relationship between satisfaction, stress, control over work and support.

Stress

Court cases in which former social workers were awarded substantial sums in damages against their employing authorities suggest that some social services staff experience intolerable levels of stress at work (North, 1996). As with lack of satisfaction, stress can affect staff commitment, efficiency, productivity, work attendance, turnover, morale and well-being (Fletcher and Payne, 1980; Cournoyer, 1988; Landy, 1989). The way in which stress is experienced, however, can be influenced by perceptions of the demands being made, the individual's ability to meet them (Landy, 1989) and the level of support available (Payne, 1979). Not all stress is harmful; limited stress can be stimulating, making work interesting, challenging, worthwhile and satisfying. Stress only begins to damage an individual's social, emotional and work life when it remains at a high and persistent level over time (Cournoyer, 1988). Unalleviated stress can weaken the immune system in the long term, increase some people's risk of infections, physical illnesses, heart disease and inevitably, sickness absence. It is possible that some individuals who are seriously affected do not realise that they are under stress (Cooper et al,1988; Landy, 1989; Qureshi and Pahl, 1992).

Stress in the Workforce studies

Staff were asked if they had experienced stress arising directly from work in year before the second interview. Table 4.2 gives details.

Table 4.2: Staff who experienced stress from work in the year before the second interview

	Percentage experiencing stress		
Job type	England	Scotland	Northern Ireland
Whole sample	62	50	31
Manager	79	87	81
Field social work staff	83	82	79
Home care worker	46	29	13
Residential worker	62	57	73
sample n	**940**	**317**	**316**

Clearly, stress was very common, and affected four out of five managers and field social work staff, and about two thirds of residential workers. There were considerable differences between categories of staff, varying from 87% of Scottish managers to 13% of home care workers in Northern Ireland. However, home care workers in England did not fare so well, with stress affecting almost half. Within each job type, a proportion of staff had not experienced stress, in spite of the fact that they would presumably have been carrying out similar tasks, suggesting that although job type is important, other factors can have an effect.

At each interview, staff were asked about sources of stress and frustration at work. Since the pattern was similar at both interviews, we will describe the more recent responses at the second interview.

Managers and field social work staff

Two thirds of managers and field social work staff were caused a 'lot' or a 'great deal' of stress by not being able to get users what they needed. Half felt that they had accountability or responsibility without power, about 40% felt out of sympathy with the way the service was run and were frustrated by game playing and office politics.

A third were affected by having to work long hours, having to take work home, uncertainty about the future, coping with the pace of change and receiving contradictory instructions. Colleagues not pulling their weight, backbiting or quarrels among staff were frustrating for a quarter, as were being overwhelmed by users' problems, feeling that their knowledge was not respected, disagreement about good practice and being harassed by managers. Situations they did not know how to deal with were stressful for a fifth, as was being on night duty for the minority to whom it applied.

Home care workers and residential workers

Not being able to get users what they needed affected up to half of residential workers and a third of home care workers, a fifth of each felt out of sympathy with the way the service was run, uncertainty about the future, coping with the pace of change and being overwhelmed by users' problems.

The greatest sources of stress for residential workers were related to team work and working with colleagues. A third were affected by backbiting, quarrels, game playing, office politics, disagreements about good practice, colleagues not pulling their weight, knowledge not being respected and having responsibility without power. In contrast, these were mentioned by fewer than a fifth of home care workers. Residential workers also experienced stress from doing night duty, working long hours, contradictory instructions, not knowing how to deal with some situations and being harassed by managers.

Very few home care workers in Northern Ireland reported stress from any source, whereas a quarter in England felt stress from uncertainty about the future, coping with the pace of change and being overwhelmed by users' problems, more than double the proportions in the other two samples.

Thus, as with dissatisfaction, most stress was caused by the aspects of the work attributable to something or somebody else, factors outside an individual's control. This was broadly in line with the findings of other studies of social care staff, for example, Thompson et al (1996) reported that stress among social workers focused on the organisational culture rather than the individual, and the stressful aspects of the work reported by Ross (1993), which included inability to influence decisions, role conflict, time pressures, heavy and emotionally demanding workloads and lack of feedback on performance.

Work was not the only source of stress. Staff with caring responsibilities for dependent adults and children have to deal with these and other home pressures on top of work. Most considered they had a good balance between work and personal time, although women and part-time staff, particularly home care workers, were more likely to say this than men or full-time staff. Generally more stress was reported from work than from home, but staff with caring responsibilities for children or adults experienced higher levels of stress than those without (Ginn and Sandell, 1997).

Staff who changed jobs, or wanted to change jobs experienced higher levels of stress. This is discussed further in Chapter Nine.

Measuring stress using the General Health Questionnaire

To identify those who were experiencing stress, we asked staff to complete the 12 item General Health Questionnaire (GHQ12) at each interview. This is one of the most extensively used instruments in surveys of this type, and is a standard measure which can be used to make comparisons with other studies. It was originally designed to detect psychiatric disorders in the general population (Goldberg, 1972; 1978), and has subsequently been used as a screening instrument for measuring stress in the workforce (Buck et al, 1994), and stress among social care staff (Gibson et al, 1989; Tobin and Carson, 1994).

The items in the GHQ12 cover various aspects of psycho–social well-being and in this analysis were scored by rating each response according to whether a symptom was absent or present, giving a maximum possible score of 12. Mean scores for groups or categories were calculated, a score of 2.00 or over indicating possible symptoms of psychological distress that a psychiatrist would recognise. Other studies have suggested that at any given time between 13% and 28% of adults in community surveys will have mean scores over 2.00 (Bowling et al, 1992).

Mean GHQ12 scores at the first and second interviews

Table 4.3 gives the mean GHQ12 scores for women and men at the first and second interviews, with the highest scores shaded. The figures quoted for Northern Ireland include mean scores for home care workers, which have the effect of substantially reducing the levels of stress reported elsewhere (McConkey et al, 1997).

Overall, stress levels were higher in England than they were in Northern Ireland or Scotland, partly due to higher scores in the two English departments which were undergoing internal reorganisation. At the second interview, mean scores had increased for English and Scottish staff, but had decreased in Northern Ireland. Although mean scores for men were higher than for women, stress levels increased at the second interview for women in England and Scotland. Not shown in the table, there were differences according to age, younger staff generally had higher scores than older staff, but against this pattern mean scores in Northern Ireland were higher for older staff. In addition, although we have given mean scores for each sample, there were wide variations between the departments and Boards taking part in the study, the mean scores for staff in at least one Northern Ireland Health Board, one of the two Scottish districts, the English county council and the inner London authority being higher than for staff elsewhere.

Table 4.3: Mean GHQ12 scores at first and second interviews

		Mean GHQ12 score	
		First interview	Second interview
Whole sample	England	2.11	2.56
	Scotland	1.66	1.94
	Northern Ireland	0.98	0.84
Women	England	1.96	2.44
	Scotland	1.56	1.77
	Northern Ireland	0.85	0.76
Men	England	3.05	3.30
	Scotland	2.56	3.20
	Northern Ireland	2.79	2.05

Job type was one of the main factors associated with stress, managers and field social work staff having higher mean scores than other staff, particularly in England and Scotland. Residential workers also experienced high levels of stress, with mean scores in each sample consistently above 2.00 at both interviews, the point at which an individual may be experiencing psychological difficulties. The table shows the very low scores for home care workers in Northern Ireland. Stress levels were higher for some categories of staff, particularly officers in charge of residential establishments, staff who worked with children and families, with users with mental health problems or severe learning difficulties.

Table 4.4 shows the mean GHQ12 scores for the four job types, with high scores shaded.

Table 4.4: Mean GHQ12 scores at first and second interviews by job type

Job type		Mean GHQ12 score	
		First interview	Second interview
Manager	England	3.28	3.57
	Scotland	2.50	3.01
	Northern Ireland	3.18	2.38
Field social work staff	England	3.17	3.24
	Scotland	3.02	3.59
	Northern Ireland	2.50	2.14
Home care worker	England	1.21	1.71
	Scotland	0.89	1.02
	Northern Ireland	0.30	0.30
Residential worker	England	2.29	2.67
	Scotland	2.40	2.43
	Northern Ireland	2.38	2.41

Differences between the two interviews show that stress may increase or decrease over time. Changes in stress levels often reflected changes in levels of satisfaction. At the second interview stress was lower while satisfaction was higher for staff in Northern Ireland, whereas staff in England, and in each sample, men, younger staff, managers, field social work staff and staff who worked with children and families had higher stress, and lower job satisfaction. This shows that the instruments for measuring satisfaction and stress are identifying related dimensions of work experience.

Stress levels in the Workforce studies were generally higher than those in a comparable survey, the British Household Panel Survey (Buck et al, 1994) in which only women managers and women intermediate non-manual workers (equivalent to women social workers) had mean scores above 2.00 (2.66 and 2.02 respectively). In fact, mean scores were higher for women than for men in each equivalent job type in the British Household Panel Study, indicating not only that stress was higher for social services staff, but also that it affects them differently from other workers.

Incidence of stress over time

Given the nature of the work, it is inevitable that some members of staff will be under pressure at any particular time, but stress levels might be expected to decline when the immediate causes have been dealt with, or have diminished. However, some staff had high levels of stress at both interviews, suggesting that the stress they were experiencing was more persistent. To examine this group, we divided the sample into four categories: those who have 'never' had scores of 2.00 or over; those who had scored 2.00 or over at the first interview only; those who had scores of 2.00 or over at the second interview only; and those who scored 2.00 or over at both interviews, the group we are concerned about. 'Never' is in quotation marks because these staff may have experienced higher stress between the interviews.

A third of staff had 'never' scored 2.00 or over, and this applied more often to women than men, partly a reflection of the high proportion of women in home care work. Two fifths of residential workers in each sample, and the same proportion of managers and field social work staff in Northern Ireland had 'never' scored 2.00 or over. However, this only applied to a quarter of managers and field social work staff in Scotland and a fifth in England. Of staff working with different user groups, this more often applied to those who worked with older people.

A third of staff had scored 2.00 or over at each interview. Although this implies that at any given time most staff did not experience stress, the proportion who had scored 2.00 or over was above the upper estimate of 28% in general population studies (Bowling et al, 1992). In addition, the proportion scoring over 2.00 was higher for most categories by the second interview.

Different individuals scored 2.00 or over at each interview, and up to two thirds of all categories of staff except home care workers had scored 2.00 or over at one interview or the other. Thus stress had affected the majority of staff at some time during the two year period covered by the study.

Details of staff who scored over 2.00 at both interviews are given in Table 4.5, with the highest proportions shaded.

Table 4.5: Staff who scored 2.00 or over in the GHQ12 at both interviews

| | Percentage who scored 2.00 or over at both interviews | | |
	England	Scotland	Northern Ireland
All	21	16	8
Gender			
Women	20	15	6
Men	31	23	23
Age at first interview			
Less than 30	33	32	14
30 to 39	26	25	12
40 to 49	18	8	9
50 or over	19	15	4
Job type first interview			
Manager	35	30	29
Social work staff	33	31	26
Home care worker	12	3	<1
Residential worker	22	31	16
User group at first interview			
Children and families	29	28	33
Older people	16	8	3
Mental health or severe learning difficulties	34	41	13
Other adults	31	32	16
Employer			
Outer London borough A	21	East 18	East 16
Midlands metropolitan borough council B	20	West 15	North 5
County council C	21		South 3
North metropolitan borough council D	20		West 18
Inner London borough E	27		
sample n	**940**	**317**	**316**

More staff in England scored 2.00 or over at both interviews than in Scotland and Northern Ireland, and in all three samples this was more likely to apply to men, managers and field social work staff. Otherwise, there were differences between categories in each sample, higher proportions of younger staff in England and Scotland, and residential workers in Scotland scored 2.00 or over at both interviews, and there were variations in each sample according to the user group and employer. In England, a higher proportion of black staff than white staff experienced high stress levels at both interviews (30% vs 20%). This was one of the few measures on which there was a difference between black and white staff.

In summary, although a minority of staff in social services experienced high levels of stress at any particular time, this proportion was higher than for other workers and some categories of staff were affected more than others. Two thirds had experienced stress at least once in this two year period, which implies that stress is potentially a problem for most staff, and is not necessarily restricted to particular individuals or groups. With the exception of home care workers, a core of about a fifth of staff experienced high levels of stress at both interviews, and this proportion rose to a third and over for some categories.

Control over work and role conflict

Having control over work, or sufficient decision latitude, is important because it enables staff to deal with demands by taking personal action (Karasek, 1979). Lack of control and role conflict are associated with dissatisfaction (Landy, 1989) and stress (Allen et al, 1990; Ross, 1993). We have already shown that two thirds of managers and field social work staff, and three quarters of home care and residential workers were satisfied with the amount of control they had. However, this suggests that between a quarter and a third were not. In the Workforce studies, control and role conflict were frequently associated with stress, for example, staff having responsibility without power, receiving contradictory instructions, being overwhelmed by users' problems and disagreement about good practice. Other research has also shown that lack of control over the work environment is one of the main causes of stress at work (Collings and Murray, 1996).

At each interview, staff were asked to respond to six statements designed to measure control and role conflict (Rizzo et al, 1970). These showed that over two thirds of managers and field social work staff felt that 'all or most of the time' they had allocated their time well, and half had done the job as they felt it should be done. However, a third had conflicting demands made of them by people in the department 'all or most of the time', a fifth were unable to do things they thought should be part of the job, 15% were expected to do things they did not think should be part of the job, and one in ten felt unclear about what they were expected to do. Responses were similar in each sample, although Scottish staff more often said they experienced conflicting demands.

Home care and residential workers responded similarly, over 90% felt they had allocated time well, and two thirds felt able to do the job as it should be done. A fifth felt that conflicting demands were made of them, and a sixth felt unable to do things that should be part of the job, were expected to do things they felt were not part of the job, or were unclear about what was expected. English and Scottish residential workers were the most likely to experience difficulties in these areas.

Responses to the six statements were summed and mean scores were calculated, giving a possible maximum score of 30, a high score representing a low level of role conflict and high control. Table 4.6 gives the mean score for each sample at the first and second interviews.

Table 4.6: Mean scores for control over work at first and second interviews

	Mean control score	
	First interview	Second interview
England	21.12	20.81
Scotland	21.23	21.30
Northern Ireland	19.54	19.76

Mean scores in England were slightly lower at the second interview and ranged from 22.12 for home care workers, who had greater control than managers, who had a score of 18.86. Mean scores in Scotland did not change, and ranged from 22.74 for staff aged over 50, who had higher control than managers whose score was 19.09. In Northern Ireland scores did not change either and ranged at the second interview from 23.76 for home care workers to 19.63 for field social work staff. Similar categories had low control in each sample, particularly men, managers, staff aged less than 40 and staff working with children and families. Control was also lower for staff working for particular employers, most notably the inner London borough and one of the four Northern Ireland Boards.

The relationship between satisfaction, control over work and stress

Since similar categories of staff experienced stress, low satisfaction and low control, it is probable that there is an association between these aspects of work. Other research has shown that satisfaction and stress are often related, lack of satisfaction can be a source of stress, while satisfaction can alleviate the effects of stress (Fletcher and Payne, 1980). The presence or absence of the same factor may either produce satisfaction or cause stress, for example, feeling valued at work might be satisfying, not feeling valued might be stressful (Beck, 1987). Workers may derive satisfaction from meeting a challenge, the challenge might be to devise a strategy to cope with stress.

Based on the mean scores in the study by Warr et al (1979), we examined the relationship between job satisfaction and stress by categorising mean scores of less than 70.00 as low satisfaction (see Table 4.1) and scores of 70.00 or over as high satisfaction. Table 4.7 gives GHQ12 scores at the second interview for staff with low and high satisfaction.

Table 4.7: Mean GHQ12 scores and satisfaction at the second interview

| | Mean GHQ12 scores at the second interview | |
	Low satisfaction	High satisfaction
England	3.65	1.68
Scotland	3.73	1.05
Northern Ireland	2.72	1.52

Table 4.7 shows that in each sample lower levels of job satisfaction were associated with higher levels of stress.

In general the most stressed workers are those who experience high demands and little decision latitude or control over their work (Karasek, 1979), although lack of control may vary in its ability to cause stress from one work setting to another (Jayaratne and Chess, 1984). As with satisfaction, the relationship between control and stress was examined by ranking the mean scores for control (see Table 4.6), scores of 18.00 or less representing low control, scores over 18.00 representing high control. Low control was associated with high stress in each sample. Mean GHQ12 scores for staff with low control were 4.40 in England, 4.10 in Scotland

and 3.95 in Northern Ireland. Mean scores for high control were 1.91 in England, 1.37 in Scotland and 1.29 in Northern Ireland.

Table 4.8 gives the GHQ12 scores at the second interview for low and high job satisfaction and low and high control over work

Table 4.8: The relationship between stress, job satisfaction and control as measured by mean GHQ12 scores at the second interview

		Mean GHQ12 scores at the second interview	
Level of control		Low satisfaction	High satisfaction
England	low	5.26	2.59
	high	2.67	1.52
Scotland	low	4.76	2.64
	high	2.84	0.90
Northern Ireland	low	4.26	3.53
	high	1.73	1.10

This table demonstrates very clearly the nature of the association between satisfaction, control over work and stress, which was replicated in each sample. Staff with low job satisfaction and low control had the highest stress levels, staff with high satisfaction and high control had the lowest stress. GHQ12 scores were lower for those who had high control and low satisfaction, and for staff who had low control and high satisfaction. This suggests that being in control or having a high level of satisfaction can be effective in reducing or alleviating stress. High satisfaction had the effect of reducing mean GHQ12 scores by up to half for staff with low control.

This association between satisfaction, control and stress was repeated at both interviews for each gender, age and ethnic category, for workers with each user group and for each job type.

Other research has shown similar relationships, that high control was associated with high personal accomplishment and satisfaction (Joseph and Conrad, 1989), particularly among medical social workers (Siefert et al, 1991), and the inverse, that workers whose jobs combine a high proportion of user contact with personal and emotional involvement may experience stress due to the worst combination, high demands and low control (Gibson et al, 1989).

Stress and time off sick

Various factors have been linked to high levels of sick leave including age and gender (Nicholson et al, 1976), staff morale, employees of large organisations taking more time off than employees of small organisations (Allen, 1982), lack of control over the work environment, and a low level of commitment to the employer (Hopkins, 1996). Studies have suggested that sick leave and stress are related, particularly for home care workers (Jones, 1989) and residential workers (Wagner, 1988). One study found that time off with stress related physical symptoms was taken for granted as a coping mechanism by social workers (Fineman, 1985).

Employers vary in the way they record time off, and the extent to which stress-related absence is reported may depend on the culture of the workplace. Since most employees are able to cope with stressful jobs without taking time off, absence through stress has often been seen as unreasonable or avoidable. However, if an employer does not accept stress as a legitimate reason for absence, employees will still stay off, but will give a different reason (Norris, 1995).

To give a context to stress and sick leave, similar proportions of staff in each job type, a majority, had excellent or very good general health, up to a quarter said their health was good, and only a minority described their health as fair or poor. These proportions compared favourably with the findings of the British Household Panel Survey (Buck et al, 1994). About a quarter of staff in each job type had a long standing illness or disability, a third of whom were affected by this daily, but very few considered themselves to be disabled, fewer than in the equivalent categories in the British Household Panel Survey, and a lower proportion were registered disabled than the minimum required of employers by the 1948 Registered Disabled Persons Act.

For the period covered by the Workforce studies, the CBI reported a mean of 8.0 days sick per annum for all employees outside local government, with 10.0 days for manual workers and 5.9 for non-manual workers. This compared with a mean for local government of 9.8 days (CBI Survey, 1994, cited in Norris, 1995). Local government manual employees had on average 10.8 days absence, non-manual workers, 7.8 days (LGMB, 1996).

Using these figures as a guide, we divided staff into two categories, those who had over 10 days self-reported sickness absence in the previous 12 months, and those who had less than this. At the first interview less than a quarter in England, and fewer than a fifth in Scotland and Northern

Ireland had taken over 10 days sick leave. By the second interview, time off sick had increased for most categories, particularly for staff over 50 in Northern Ireland and residential workers, and in some cases the proportions had increased dramatically, doubling for residential workers in Scotland. Similar categories of staff to those in the CBI and LGMB surveys had high numbers of days off sick in each sample, including, at the second interview, a third of staff aged less than 30, a third of manual workers (broadly home care and residential workers), and up to a third of women staff in England.

It was very unusual for the same individuals to have had more than 10 days off before both interviews. In England, this applied to only 11% of staff, compared with 59% who had taken 10 or less days off before both interviews. In Scotland the respective figures were 7% and 64%, in Northern Ireland, 4% and 68%.

In summary, sick leave in the Workforce studies followed the pattern of sick leave in other sectors. Higher proportions of manual workers than non-manual workers had over 10 days off but it was unusual for the same individuals to have this amount of time off prior to both interviews. The categories of staff with over 10 days sick leave were similar to those with low satisfaction and high stress. However, there were two exceptions, women, especially home care workers, who had lower stress than men but had more time off sick, and managers, who had higher stress, but less time off sick than the other job types.

At the second interview staff were asked if they had taken sick leave in the last 12 months due to stress arising from work. Very few had, 7% in England, 3% in Scotland and 2% in Northern Ireland, although men were more likely to than women, particularly in Northern Ireland, where 11% of men had been off through stress compared with 2% of women.

We examined this further by calculating the mean GHQ12 scores for staff who had more than 10 days sick before the second interview, and for staff who had less than this. Mean scores were higher for every category of staff with more than 10 days sick leave, except managers in Northern Ireland, showing that although staff themselves reported very little stress-related sick leave, there was a very clear association between stress and increased time off. However, this may indicate that stress is associated with being ill, not just with the number of days off sick. Table 4.9 gives mean GHQ12 scores at the second interview for staff who described their health as fair or poor, for staff who had taken time off because of work-related stress, and for staff who reported both of these.

Table 4.9: Mean GHQ12 scores at the second interview for health and stress-related sick leave

	Mean GHQ12 score at second interview*		
	England	Scotland	Northern Ireland
Health last 12 months Fair or poor	4.58	3.23	3.63
Excellent/very good/good	2.16	1.72	2.23
Sick leave for work-related stress+ Yes	6.44	2.86	4.87
No	2.63	2.22	2.14
Poor health and sick leave for stress+	8.08	7.68	6.50

* Figures exclude Northern Ireland home care workers.
+ Of those those who had time off sick.

GHQ12 scores were higher among staff whose health was fair or poor, and for staff who had taken sick leave because of work-related stress, although this association was not as strong for staff in Scotland and Northern Ireland. As might be expected, GHQ12 scores were very high for staff with poor health who had taken sick leave for stress.

Support

A minority of staff, between a third and a half depending on the job type, said there were established ways in their team or workplace for dealing with stress arising from their work with users. Most staff, particularly field social work staff and home care workers in Scotland, either said there were no established ways, or they did not know if there were. Overall, about half felt they had enough support from others at work in dealing with stress.

A quarter of home care workers and a fifth of managers, field social work staff and residential workers said they did not need support in dealing with stress, or did not feel stress. Half of managers and field social work staff, and a third of residential workers said colleagues and co-workers were the most important source of support. English managers and a quarter of other staff said friends or family outside work were the most important. One in 10 managers, field social work staff and residential workers, dealt with stress themselves or did not involve anyone else, others found support from elsewhere in the department, or from other professional contacts. Only one in 10 staff said their manager or supervisor was the most important source of support, a surprising finding, since this is one of the main roles for managers and supervisors.

As an illustration of the importance of support in dealing with stress, Table 4.10 gives the mean GHQ12 scores for staff who did and did not have enough support. Cells are shaded where scores were higher.

Table 4.10: Support in dealing with stress: mean GHQ12 scores at second interview

| | Mean GHQ12 scores | | | | | |
| | England | | Scotland | | Northern Ireland | |
	Enough	Not enough	Enough	Not enough	Enough	Not enough
All	1.75	4.34	1.32	3.48	0.74	2.40
Managers	2.21	5.31	2.25	4.13	1.26	4.74
Field social work staff	2.06	4.93	3.18	3.80	1.78	2.62
Home care workers	1.44	3.01	0.22	3.02	0.27	0.62
Residential workers	1.80	4.45	1.57	3.62	1.35	3.79

Scores for every category who did not have enough support in dealing with stress were double the scores of those who had enough. In particular, the table identifies, unusually, a group of home care workers in England and Scotland who had high GHQ12 scores.

Table 4.11 gives mean satisfaction scores according to whether or not enough support was received. Lowest scores, indicating low satisfaction, are shaded.

Table 4.11: Support in dealing with stress: mean satisfaction scores at second interview

| | Mean satisfaction scores and support | | | | | |
| | England | | Scotland | | Northern Ireland | |
	Enough	Not enough	Enough	Not enough	Enough	Not enough
All	74.14	61.05	77.93	61.45	74.67	68.40
Managers	73.25	62.88	71.65	62.21	74.42	64.80
Field social work staff	70.17	56.80	73.47	60.98	72.60	67.24
Home care workers	75.84	66.29	81.70	66.14	75.17	72.23
Residential workers	74.68	57.52	77.77	53.45	76.09	65.02

Satisfaction was much lower for every category of staff who did not receive enough support. Levels were extremely low for managers, field social work staff and residential workers in England and Scotland.

In addition to the association with stress and satisfaction, staff who did not have enough support were more likely to have had more than ten days sick, and were likely to have a lower level of control.

Conclusions

Most social services staff experience high levels of satisfaction from their work. Staff find most satisfaction from aspects of work over which they have most control, activities that produce rewards from their own efforts. The least satisfaction came from aspects of the work over which they had little control, particularly those relating to the organisation. Although there were staff with low satisfaction in every category, it was particularly a problem for men, younger staff, managers and field social work staff, those working with children and families, and staff working for particular employers.

Stress was also associated with aspects of the work over which staff have least control, often the aspects associated with the least satisfaction. Most stress was caused by lack of resources and inability to provide the standard of service staff would like to provide. Several factors were associated with stress, in particular, low job satisfaction and low control over work, and although very few staff took time off sick because of stress, there was a clear association between high GHQ12 scores, poor health and increased sick leave. As with low satisfaction, stress affected higher proportions of men, managers, field social work staff and residential workers, staff working with children and families, or users with mental health problems or severe learning difficulties. Stress was more likely to have been experienced at one interview only, but in the two years of the study it had affected two thirds of all staff. Proportions had risen by the second interview for most categories of staff, and more seriously, a fifth had experienced high levels of stress at both interviews.

Stress may affect different people at different times and it is often the result of temporary circumstances. During the Workforce studies, stress in some departments may have been exacerbated by the reorganisation of services, with high levels of threatened and actual redundancies. Stress will be reduced or alleviated for at least a proportion of staff when circumstances change, but it is not possible to prevent its recurrence through other circumstances. We have shown that having control over work can be effective in reducing stress and increasing job satisfaction. Thus, although stress may be an intrinsic part of the job, it may therefore be possible to alleviate it through job redesign, giving staff more control or decision latitude, enabling them to deal with demands by taking personal action (Karasek, 1979).

Although there is a role for education and training, it is clearly important to look at work routines, job content and daily practice. Staff may not realise that they are experiencing stress, or may feel that they do not have time to undertake training because pressures are too great. Yet these pressures may partly be due to unproductive work practices such as the inability to prioritise or delegate, or the fear that users may be let down. Staff may also fear that by saying they are experiencing stress, they may expose themselves to unfavourable judgement, be seen as unable to cope with the work and unsuitable for promotion. Ironically, staff who do not discuss these issues and take up training opportunities may be the people who need to do this most.

Only one person in 10 said the most important support for dealing with stress was their manager or supervisor, the person specifically paid to provide support. Staff who felt they did not have enough support had higher stress and lower satisfaction levels, indicating either that lack of support is stressful and dissatisfying, or that staff who experience stress and low satisfaction need more support. Staff are bound to feel frustrated and dissatisfied if they cannot influence decisions, if there are too many deadlines, too little time to carry out work, if their contribution is not valued, if they are not given feedback, if good work is not recognised, and if there are limited rewards in terms of pay and promotion. Many of these issues can be resolved within existing structures. There is potential for managers and supervisors to be involved in identifying staff who are experiencing difficulties at work, and in providing support through formal supervision and other means. Staff can be supported by appraising their strengths and weaknesses by developing the more interesting and challenging aspects of the job, by developing strategies to increase control over work, by learning to improve workload management and by participation in decision making.

These are important findings. The social services workforce has been a committed, stable and mature one, and while this stability may have enabled staff to cope with stressful aspects of the job in the past, it would appear that this may no longer be the case for everyone. If stress levels are rising and satisfaction is reduced, the stability and cohesion which has ensured continuity and quality of service may be threatened. Quite apart from the effect on individuals, stress can also affect staff's response to users and their ability to make decisions; social services' users lives can be irreversibly affected by, among other things, decisions about reception of children and adults into care, the follow up of suspected child abuse, and compulsory detention in a psychiatric hospital.

Increasing levels of stress may not be inevitable if staff are supported in dealing with it. However, the consequences of failing to tackle stress are poorer performance, poorer quality of service, high levels of sickness absence, and as will be shown in Chapter Nine, staff wanting to leave.

FIVE

Coping with physical violence and verbal abuse

Jan Pahl

Physical violence and verbal abuse were drawn to our attention by the people who took part in this study. These were not topics which we had planned to investigate, and indeed, they were barely mentioned in the original proposal for the research (Qureshi and Pahl, 1992). However, both in the qualitative interviews carried out at the pilot stage, and in the first interviews, physical violence, threats of violence and verbal abuse were mentioned so frequently that the topic became the subject of a section of our first report (Balloch et al, 1995, pp 58-65). When the team began planning the questionnaire for the second interviews, a series of questions was included which would allow the topic to be explored in more detail.

The Health and Safety at Work Act of 1974 makes it clear that employers must be concerned about these issues. The Act lays a general duty on an employer, 'to ensure, so far as is reasonably practicable, the health, safety and welfare of all his employees'. More specifically the Act includes among the responsibilities of an employer the following duties:

- The provision and maintenance of plant and systems of work that are, so far as is reasonably practicable, safe and without risk to health.
- The provision of such information, instruction, training and supervision as is necessary to ensure, so far as is reasonably practicable, the health and safety at work of employees.
- The provision and maintenance of a working environment for employees that is, so far as is reasonably practicable, safe and without risk to health.

The Management of Health and Safety at Work Regulations of 1992 require all employers to assess the risks to the health and safety of their staff. This is in order to identify, and put into place, appropriate preventive and protective measures. The measures should cover planning, organisation, control, monitoring and review. Guidance on carrying out a risk assessment has been produced by the Health and Safety Executive (HSE, 1975; 1990; 1995).

Employers also have a general duty of care towards their staff under common law, and this includes the risk of violence at work. Legal precedents, such as *West Bromwich Building Society v Townsend (1983)* and *Charlton v Forrest Printing Ink Company (1980)* show that employers have a duty to see that their staff are not exposed to unnecessary risks at work, including the risk of injury by violent criminals (HSE, 1995).

The Health and Safety at Work Act created a framework for our questions. To what extent do social services departments provide an environment which is safe for their employees? Are some environments more dangerous, and some employees more at risk, than others? What are the circumstances in which violent attacks or abuse take place? And what help or support do employees receive when they have been attacked or threatened with attack?

Background to the topic

Recent research has made it clear that violence at work affects many different occupations, and that employers in many different sectors are becoming aware of their responsibility to provide a safe working environment. So, for example, reports have been produced on violence against librarians (Library Association, 1987), general practitioners (D'Urso and Hobbs, 1989), staff in banks and building societies (HSE, 1993), nurses (Royal College of Nursing, 1994) and retail staff (HSE, 1995). The Suzy Lamplugh Trust has done much to raise awareness of violence at work and to develop training programmes for staff. A research review prepared for the Trust concluded that:

- Violence at work is an issue for both employers and employees.
- It is widespread, and not confined to 'women's work' or to the UK.
- It has high costs, both to the individual and to the organisation.
- Young men are the group most vulnerable to physical attack.
- Organisational action is crucial to creating a safer workplace.
  (Phillips et al, 1989)

There is evidence that violence at work is increasing. The 1992 British Crime Survey showed that violent assaults at work doubled between 1981 and 1991, compared with a slight fall in violence in the street or in pubs and clubs. This may partly reflect the fact that workers have become more likely to identify such assaults as violent crime, and more likely to report them to managers – or researchers. The British Crime Survey also showed that nurses and 'welfare workers' were three times more likely than the average employee to be physically attacked or threatened (Mayhew et al, 1993).

A number of studies has provided more detailed evidence about the nature and extent of violence in the social services. Most of these studies have been concerned with violence against social workers, as opposed to other groups of staff. The results suggest that a great many social workers are attacked or threatened in the course of their work. Thus a postal survey carried out in Wessex in 1979 suggested that 29% of respondents had been assaulted at least once in the last three years, while 40% had been threatened with assault; in all 53% had experienced violence or threats of violence. Threats and attacks were more common in residential establishments than in field work settings (Brown et al, 1986).

In the past many incidents were never reported, partly because social workers tended to blame themselves for what happened and partly because, when incidents were reported, the response from management was not seen as supportive. Thus a retrospective study carried out by Surrey Social Services Department among residential staff showed that approximately a third of respondents had not reported attacks to their line managers, while two thirds had not recorded the attack on an incident form (Crane, 1986; Rowett, 1986; Surrey County Council, 1987; Hayes and Glastonbury, 1989; King, 1989; Norris with Kedward, 1990; Bibby, 1994).

There were two main limitations to existing knowledge about violence in the social services. First, most of the studies were focused on social workers, while other groups of staff, such as managers or care assistants, were relatively neglected in the existing literature; this was despite the fact that social workers make up only about ten per cent of the social services workforce (LGMB, 1996). Second, most of the studies were limited, either in terms of the geographical areas involved or in terms of the size of the sample. Some were introduced to respondents as studies of violence, which may have led to a bias in the sample, because they stimulated a higher response rate from those who had experienced violence.

The NISW Workforce studies offered an opportunity to overcome some of these limitations. They covered a wider range of social services employees than any previous study, drawn from many different parts of the country, and investigated violence, not in a specialised study, but in the course of an interview which covered many other topics. The studies were timely in that they offered an opportunity to find out whether appropriate responses had been put in place by employers and managers following the various guidelines which had been produced in the late 1980s (DoH, 1988).

The disparity in size between the samples in England, Scotland and Northern Ireland means that pooling the three data sets would mean that the English data dominated the results. In this chapter data from the three samples are usually presented separately, though for some of the more detailed analyses English data is used, with variations in Scotland and Northern Ireland being noted where appropriate.

The experience of violence

Vivid evidence about the experience of violence was provided in the qualitative interviews which were carried out in the pilot stage of the study and in the telephone interviews. There is space here to quote the words of just one person, the officer in charge of a residential home for teenagers. She described an incident in which a 16-year-old boy,

> ... **punched a female member of staff. I intervened and got bitten and head-butted, but held on till the police came ... nose bleeding, lip swollen. The young boy was held overnight in custody and released the next morning. It's unlikely there will even be a charge, because he's not an offender, he has no criminal record. So he's unlikely to be charged with assault times two. He's likely to be just cautioned for it. He's not remorseful; he's threatening and abusive, both physically and verbally, to members of staff.**

When asked what support was available to staff who had been assaulted, she replied,

> **We de-brief each other; we support each other; there's no place to go. When I worked in the voluntary sector if you were faced with an aggressive or violent incident you filled out your report and you were automatically referred to the violence and aggression [support service]. There was a person employed to deal with this, and they would contact you and make an**

appointment and talk it through with you. It was compulsory .... [Here] we have no specific place to go and no specific person to go to. Two years ago we went out [on strike] for twelve days for violence and management's response to our request for help, which helped things along for a year, and then it's all slipped the other way again.

Individual accounts such as this raise questions about the broader picture. How common is this woman's experience, in terms of the location in which it took place, the types of people involved and the response of more senior colleagues? In order to answer these questions we turn now to the quantitative data from the NISW study.

The nature and extent of violence

At the first interview respondents were asked about the extent to which they had experienced violence in their current jobs. The results are shown in Table 5.1, which brings together actual violence, threats of violence and verbal abuse. The data show that violence, threats of violence and verbal abuse are very much part of the working lives of those employed by social services and social work departments: about three quarters of all those who took part in the survey had been shouted at or insulted in the course of their current jobs.

However, Table 5.1 suggests that the three samples were similar in terms of the overall levels of violence and abuse, but that there were significant differences between job types within samples. Home care staff were the least likely to report having been physically attacked or threatened with violence, though two thirds had been subject to verbal abuse. By contrast, the great majority of residential workers had experienced physical violence, of which the quotation above is an example. Residential staff in Scotland were particularly at risk. Table 5.1 shows that 72% of residential workers in the two districts sampled in Scotland had been physically attacked in their present jobs, compared with 12% of home care workers in Scotland, and 62% of residential workers in England. Social work staff (field workers in Scotland) were more likely than other staff groups to have been shouted at, insulted or threatened, without actually being attacked; this may be a reflection of their very real power, which can provoke service users and their relatives to abuse, but which also protects them to some extent from more serious physical attack.

Table 5.1: Experience of physical attack, threats and verbal abuse in current job: percentages of respondents at first interview by job type and sample

	All	Managers	Field social work staff	Home care workers	Residential workers
Physical attack					
England	34	32	23	19	62
Scotland	30	44	28	12	72
Northern Ireland	–	32	23	–	64
Threats of violence					
England	34	44	46	14	53
Scotland	34	54	55	13	66
Northern Ireland	–	40	45	–	75
Shouted at/insulted					
England	73	71	82	64	82
Scotland	75	87	78	67	90
Northern Ireland	–	73	81	–	87

Note: For some analyses home care staff in Northern Ireland were omitted.

These results were so striking that the second interviews included a series of more detailed questions about violence and abuse. The original question was reworded to focus on the last twelve months (rather than in their current jobs) while retaining a broad definition of violence. All those who took part in the survey were asked, 'In the last 12 months, have service users or their relatives attacked you or physically abused you, threatened to attack you, shouted at you or insulted you, or done none of these?' Table 5.2 shows the results for England and Scotland. Again the table highlights the very high rates of violence experienced by staff working in residential homes, and especially by those working in Scotland. More than half of Scottish residential workers had experienced a physical attack over the previous year, compared with under a third of residential workers in England, and on nearly every measure staff in the Scottish sample experienced more violent behaviour than staff in England. The reason for the higher rates of violence in Scotland are unclear. One explanation may be that the two districts where the research took place were both in large cities, while in England the research took place in five rather different types of environment. The English data showed that staff in the two London boroughs experienced rather higher levels of violence than staff in the three other authorities involved in the study.

Table 5.2: Experience of physical attack, threats and verbal abuse in past 12 months: percentages of respondents at second interview by job type and sample

	Managers	Field social work staff	Home care workers	Residential workers
Physical attack				
England	16	10	2	29
Scotland	18	19	1	58
Threats of violence				
England	19	29	5	29
Scotland	29	32	2	49
Shouted at/insulted				
England	49	61	28	57
Scotland	56	65	25	60
None of the above				
England	44	36	72	38
Scotland	42	28	73	26

The interview continued with a series of questions about the 'most recent' violent or abusive incident. We hoped that focusing on the 'most recent' incident would provide us with a snapshot view of the nature of the violence which takes place in social services and social work departments. It is important to remember that this approach does not tell us about the frequency with which different sorts of violence take place, though it does give a picture of the typical range of violent incidents. In reporting the picture we draw mainly on the data from the English survey, reporting results from Scotland and Northern Ireland when these were substantially different.

Violence and abusive incidents had taken place in a variety of different locations, with the most common being in the building where the member of staff worked (44% in the English survey), in a service user's home (35%), or in the staff member's own office (12%). The majority of incidents had taken place during the day, with the most dangerous time being late morning, but 16% of incidents had taken place in the evening, and 9% at night.

What was happening when the incident took place, and who was involved? We offered staff a list of possibilities and asked them to select the one which best described the most recent violent or abusive incident. Most commonly staff in England said that they were simply 'on duty'

(39% of incidents) or 'providing personal care' (31%); other circumstances in which violent incidents took place included interviewing a service user or relative (11% of incidents), giving advice (9%) and doing an assessment (5%). Carrying out the provisions of the 1989 Children Act or the 1983 Mental Health Act gave rise to relatively few of the 'most recent' violent incidents, but this probably reflected the fact that relatively few of the incidents involved social work staff.

In nearly a quarter of 'most recent' incidents in England the person responsible was the relative of a service user, rather than service users themselves. When the person responsible for the 'most recent' incident was a service user, he or she was most likely to be an older person, either living at home (23% of incidents) or in residential care (14%). Other groups of service users mentioned as being responsible for the 'most recent' incident included adults with mental health problems (15%), children and young people (14%) and adults with severe learning difficulties (11%). These results must be treated with some caution, since the frequency of the 'most recent' incidents is partly a reflection of the representation of particular job types and service users in the sample: so staff who worked with older people were well-represented in the sample, compared, for example, with staff who worked with drug and alcohol dependency. However, in Scotland drug and alcohol dependants were prominent among those who inflicted violence, partly because they were well-represented in the sample.

What actually happened when the violent incident took place? In the English sample 317 people reported at least one incident involving physical violence, threat of violence or verbal abuse in the past twelve months. Although the great majority of these took the form of verbal abuse or shouting, 64 involved the member of staff being kicked, hit or bitten and 40 involved him or her being pushed, grabbed or shoved; in 25 incidents the member of staff was slapped, in 10 something was thrown, and in three she or he was threatened with a gun or knife.

Patterns of violence and abuse

In order to be able to make suggestions about appropriate responses it was necessary to know more about the patterns of violence and abuse. Which members of staff were most at risk, and in what circumstances did they experience violence or threats?

The questions about the 'most recent' incident were used to build up a picture of the typical pattern of violence experienced by each group of staff. For *managers*, the 'most recent' incident was likely to have taken place in the buildings where they worked, but not necessarily in their own offices. It is important to remember the variety of jobs within the general category of 'manager'. Senior managers experienced very little violence of any sort, but for the managers of residential homes violence was a common occurrence (For further information on this issue see Balloch et al, 1998.) Some managers in residential settings were attacked when they went to the help of other members of staff, as occurred in the quotation earlier in this chapter. The most common activity at the time when the incident took place was described simply as being 'on duty'. This was the group which was most likely to be attacked, not by service users, but by their relatives, with 38% of 'most recent' acts of violence against managers in England being made by relatives, as opposed to 22% for the sample as a whole.

Field social work staff were the job type most likely to have experienced violence in their own offices, so that in England 30% of 'most recent' incidents took place here, as opposed to 12% for the English sample as a whole; in addition 34% of incidents affecting social work staff took place in the homes of service users. When the 'most recent' violent incident took place, social work staff were more likely than other job types to be interviewing service users, carrying out assessments or giving advice, a pattern which reflects the nature of their work. The time of day of the 'most recent' incident also reflected patterns of work, with managers and social work staff typically being at greatest risk during the afternoon, as Table 5.3 shows.

For *home care staff* the 'most recent' incident had typically taken place in the home of a service user, 88% of incidents falling into this category, compared with 35% for the sample as a whole. Abuse was more likely to be verbal than physical in both England and Scotland. Typically the incident took place in the course of providing personal care and had involved a service user rather than a relative, which may reflect the fact that people living alone tend to have priority for receiving home care. Compared with other staff groups, home care staff were at greatest risk in the mornings, the time when much of home care work is carried out.

For *residential workers* the 'most recent' incident, not surprisingly, had taken place in the building where they worked and in the course of providing personal care. Almost all incidents had involved service users, with only 5% initiated by relatives. In general, as we have seen, these were often quite serious. When describing the 'most recent' incident, residential workers were far more likely than other job types to mention being pushed, slapped, grabbed, hit, kicked or bitten, and to say that the number of incidents was 'too many to count'. The frightening nature of these incidents must have been exacerbated by the fact that many took place at times when relatively few staff were on duty; for example, in England 44% of these 'most recent' incidents took place in the evening or at night, compared with only 14% of the incidents reported by social work staff.

Table 5.3: Time of day when 'most recent' violent incident occurred: percentages by job type in England

Time of day	Managers	Social work staff	Home care workers	Residential workers
Early morning	22	4	31	21
Later in the morning	22	37	44	19
Afternoon	35	44	10	16
Evening	15	8	14	24
Night-time	4	6	1	20
sample n	155	134	77	126

For all our sample the 'most recent' incident was more likely to involve an older person than any other type of service user. This was largely because older people made up the largest single group of social service users, and because a majority of our panel worked with this group. However, when we explored the extent to which different user groups had been 'violence prone' in the previous 12 months a different picture emerged, as Table 5.4 shows. This table presents data for England and Northern Ireland only, and shows that staff who worked with older people and people with physical disabilities were more likely than others to have escaped violence altogether.

Table 5.4 suggests that, in general, staff in England reported more violence over the previous twelve months than staff in Northern Ireland; however, the numbers for the latter were quite small, so caution is needed in interpreting these results. Service users with mental health problems or learning difficulties were more likely to be physically violent than any other group. Children and young people were more likely to shout at, or verbally abuse, staff. More detailed analyses for Scotland suggested that violence by children and young people came mainly from children and young people in care, rather than from young offenders.

Table 5.4: Types of violence experienced in the past 12 months: percentages by type of service user in England and Northern Ireland

	Children and young people		Older people		Mental health and learning difficulties		Physical and other disability	
	England	Northern Ireland	England	Northern Ireland	England	Northern Ireland	England	Northern Ireland
Physical attack	5	15	7	7	38	7	15	0
Threats of violence	44	16	9	7	40	12	20	29
Shouted at or insulted	77	33	40	39	64	45	51	21
None of the above	21	36	58	46	30	36	41	50

Staff working with different user groups also had different experiences in terms of whether a service user or a relative inflicted the violence. Most violence and abuse came from service users, but relatives were responsible for 16% of incidents in Scotland, 23% of incidents in England and a third of incidents in Northern Ireland. However, the extent to which relatives were involved varied according to job type and user group. Relatives were the protagonists in 23% of incidents in England, but this rose to 28% when a child or a young person was concerned. In Scotland about a third of all attacks on managers and field social work staff were by relatives compared with only a tenth of attacks on home care and residential workers.

Dangerous times of day for staff also differed according to the user group, and the pattern we found seemed to conjure up a vivid picture of the times of greatest volatility. For example, in England 22% of 'most recent' incidents took place in the evening or at night, but when the staff member worked with children or young people, 30% of incidents took place at these times. For those who worked with older people, first thing in the morning was a more dangerous time, with 28% of incidents taking place then, as opposed to 19% for the sample as a whole.

To what extent did gender, age or ethnicity make a person more vulnerable to physical attack and abuse? We carried out a series of analyses to examine the extent to which these factors were related to the experience of violence, threats of violence or verbal abuse over the last twelve months. The results showed that in general men were more likely than women to have experienced all the different types of violence. This was partly because home care staff were more likely to be female and less likely to experience violence, but even when home care staff were excluded, the gender effect remained. Table 5.5, which shows the figures for England only, underlines the significant relationship between gender and having experienced different types of violence in the last 12 months. Thus a fifth of men had experienced physical attack, compared with a tenth of women.

Table 5.5: Violence and gender: percentages experiencing different types of violence in the past 12 months in England

	Men	Women
Physical attack	21	11
Threats of violence	30	16
Shouted at or insulted	59	42
sample n	**297**	**643**

There are many possible reasons for the greater vulnerability of male staff. It could be that, compared with female staff, they are more likely to be asked to intervene in potentially dangerous situations; service users may perceive male staff as more challenging and provocative, or female members of staff may be more skilled at deflecting and defusing violence.

There also seemed to be a relationship between age and the experience of violence, with younger staff being more vulnerable than older staff in all three samples. There were various possible explanations for this. Service users may have been more likely to attack younger than older workers and older workers may have developed skills in handling and diverting violent behaviour. On the other hand, the reason could simply have been that older workers were in managerial or other jobs where there was less contact with service users.

Black and Asian members of staff did not experience more violence and abuse than white staff. However, when they took place such attacks were more likely to have a racist focus than was the case when white staff were involved (see also Chapter Six). There was a slight tendency for staff from ethnic minorities who worked in the two London boroughs to experience more threats and verbal abuse than staff who worked in the three other local authorities involved in the English study.

In order to disentangle the effects of different variables on the risk of experiencing violence we carried out a regression analysis on the English data. The detailed results are reported elsewhere (Balloch et al, 1998). The analysis focused on the risk of physical violence in the current job and examined the effects of job type, service user group, length of time in the current job, gender, age and ethnicity. The results showed that residential workers were four times as likely to be attacked as managers or social work staff. Men were more than twice as likely to be attacked as women, and those who worked with people with mental health problems or learning difficulties were twice as likely to be attacked as those working with other service users. The regression analysis suggested that when other factors were taken into account, age, ethnicity and length of time in the current job did not significantly affect a person's chances of being attacked.

Comparisons with other occupational groups

Clearly working in the social services presents hazards: but are those who work in this field more likely to experience violence or abuse than other professionals? As we have seen, there has been an increasing concern about violence at work, and a number of recent empirical studies have made comparisons possible. The 1988 British Crime Survey included new questions about crime at work, which provided evidence about the relative risks of working in different occupations. This showed that nurses and 'welfare workers' were three times more likely than the average employee to be physically attacked or threatened; teachers were also particularly vulnerable, but in their case threats and verbal abuse were more likely than physical assaults. Other occupational groups with an increased risk of violence included managers in the entertainment sector, security guards and female office managers (Mayhew et al, 1989, p 35).

Further evidence has come from studies of violence in specific occupations. The most relevant comparisons seemed to be with general medical practice and with different types of nursing (D'Urso and Hobbs, 1989; Harris, 1989; Royal College of Nursing, 1994). As Table 5.6 shows, in the course of a year physical attacks are likely to occur to 7% of community and district nurses, 6% of school nurses, and 5% of health visitors, practice nurses and community psychiatric nurses; general practitioners seem less vulnerable to violence, with only 3% being physically attacked and 23% verbally abused in the course of a year.

Table 5.6: Violence in different occupations: percentages experiencing types of violence in the past 12 months

	Physical attack	Threats of violence	Verbal abuse
Community/district nurses*	7	12	81
School nurses*	6	3	91
Health visitors	5	24	71
Practice nurses*	5	7	88
Community psychiatric nurses*	5	30	65
General practitioners**	3	4	23
Field social work staff			
England	10	29	61
Scotland	19	32	65
Northern Ireland	5	13	48
Residential workers			
England	29	29	57
Scotland	58	49	60
Northern Ireland	29	32	64

Sources: *Royal College of Nursing (1994); **Harris (1989). All other data taken from the NISW Workforce studies.

Table 5.6 underlines the fact that working for social services or for a social work department does represent a relatively dangerous occupational choice, particularly in England and Scotland. Social care is more dangerous than any health service profession, in terms of violence and threats of violence, with the possible exception of community psychiatric nursing, and working in residential social care, particularly with young people, is much more dangerous, exposing the employee to even higher levels of physical violence and threats of violence. Verbal abuse seems to be a relatively common experience for those who work in health and social care, except for general practitioners.

Action in response to violence and abuse

Finally, it seemed important to know how violence affected staff, what support they had received from the departments for which they worked, and what more could be done to ameliorate the problem of violence in social services. In this section of the interview we repeated questions which had been asked of the same people two years previously, because we were interested to see how things had changed over this period. Table 5.7 gives data for England and shows what those who experienced violence and abuse said about how they had been affected, with the answers from the first interviews in brackets.

Table 5.7: Effect of 'most recent' incident on staff: percentages by job type in England (first interview figures from Balloch et al, [1995] in brackets)

Staff were affected	Managers	Social work staff	Home care workers	Residential workers
Very much/quite a lot	27 (28)	42 (52)	39 (41)	25 (28)
Just a little	46 (56)	42 (31)	46 (37)	34 (42)
Not at all	27 (25)	16 (16)	16 (16)	42 (30)

Table 5.7 suggests that there may have been some real improvement in the extent to which staff are affected by violence and abuse. In particular social work staff were less inclined to say that they had been 'very much' affected by the violence, and residential workers were more likely to say that they had not been affected at all. However, these changes could also reflect the alteration in the question, since the first interview asked about incidents in the person's 'current job' while the second asked about incidents in 'the last 12 months'. But it may also be that the publicity given to the issue, and the efforts that have been made to protect staff and to reduce violence, have had some effect.

Comparable data was provided by the 1992 British Crime Survey, which asked victims of crime to rate how much violent incidents had affected them. The results showed that in general work-based crime is less upsetting than other types of crime, but that it distresses women more than men. So 11% of men and 17% of women said that they had been 'very much affected' by incidents of violence at work (Mayhew et al, 1993). In the NISW survey the extent to which staff were affected by violence did not differ significantly according to gender, age or ethnicity. However, there were differences according to job type.

The extent to which violence was upsetting seemed to vary in inverse relationship to the frequency with which violence occurred. Thus those who experienced violence more often, such as residential workers, seemed to find it less upsetting. It may also be that people who usually work on their own and who have to go into people's homes in the course of their work, such as social work staff and home care workers, feel more vulnerable and find violence more distressing; by contrast, residential workers usually have colleagues there when violence occurs and are more likely to feel supported.

What did workers feel about the help and support given to them by their employers in dealing with the emotional effects of violence and abuse? We asked members of staff to assess the help which they had received in response to the 'most recent' incident. The results are shown in Table 5.8.

Table 5.8: Help provided by employers in dealing with the effects of violence: percentages by job type and sample

	Managers	Field social work staff	Home care workers	Residential workers
Right amount of help*				
England	50	52	70	45
Scotland	61	48	39	45
Northern Ireland	36	46	–	43
Less help than necessary**				
England	41	41	19	46
Scotland	37	50	46	46
Northern Ireland	44	43	–	45
No help available				
England	9	7	11	7
Scotland	2	2	14	9
Northern Ireland	21	11	–	12

*'Right amount of help' includes 'more help available than needed' and 'no help sought'.

** 'Less help than necessary' includes 'somewhat less help' and 'a lot less help'.

Table 5.8 suggests that there was still much that managers in social services and social work departments could be doing to help employees who have experienced violence or abuse. Though over half of the sample felt that they had received the right amount of help, substantial minorities had received a lot less help than they considered necessary. Field social workers in Scotland were particularly likely to feel that they had received less help than necessary, while in Northern Ireland 21% of managers and 12% of residential staff said that no help was available for them.

In the course of the second interview staff were asked about the training courses which they had attended during the previous year, and some mentioned that they had had training to help them to cope with violence and its effects. The numbers involved were very small, but it seemed as if training had not always gone to those who might be thought to need it most. For example, in the English survey women were more likely than men to have attended training courses, despite the fact that men were more likely to have experienced violence and abuse. Few of the staff working in the two London boroughs had attended training courses on this topic, despite the fact that workers in London seemed more likely to experience threats and verbal abuse than workers in the three other English local authorities. However, it was reassuring to find that residential workers were more likely than any other job type to have been on training courses on violence and abuse.

Over the past few years a number of publications have been produced with the aim of helping employers to prevent violence, to protect staff and to support them when violence has occurred (see, for example, DoH, 1988; Owens and Keville, 1990; Rowett and Breakwell, 1992; Bibby, 1994; Kinney, 1995; Leadbetter and Trewartha, 1996). In addition many local authorities have developed their own policies and procedures for dealing with violence.

There is only space here to summarise some of the main recommendations. Since 1992 there has been a legal requirement on employers to assess risks in the workplace. The Health and Safety Executive has suggested that the best way to tackle violence is through a seven point action plan, with the following steps.

- **Find out if there is a problem, by asking the staff involved**
- **Record all incidents, and encourage employees to report incidents**
- **Classify all incidents, to identify dangerous times, places and circumstances**
- **Search for appropriate preventive and protective measures**
- **Consult all employees about proposed safety measures**
- **Put measures into practice and publicise the policy**
- **Check that the measures are working and reassess regularly**

(HSE 1988)

Despite all these steps violence and abuse will continue to occur. Useful guidelines on the after-care of social services staff who have experienced violence are given by Bibby (1994). She suggests that people who have experienced violence or abuse often need to talk through the incident with a 'de-briefer', and some need long-term counselling. It may be appropriate for staff to have time off work to recover, either physically or emotionally, and their earnings should be protected during this time. Safety precautions should include the protection of staff when they go home, if relevant. Police involvement, and legal action, may be appropriate in some cases, and all employers should carry insurance to cover the death or injury of employees.

Conclusions

The causes of the violence experienced by those who work for social services and social work departments are many and tangled. On the one hand, violence reminds us that social care is about control as well as care. For many service users their experience of social care involves frustration and disappointment, and their response is to lash out at those whom they perceive to be responsible. On the other hand, even when social care is about responding to needs, the limits on what can be provided make rationing inevitable. For people who already experience life as hard and difficult, setting limits to what is offered can create resentment towards those who appear to be the gatekeepers to the system. The reality is that social care staff work at some crucial boundaries between individuals and the state, and that the criteria about who can cross those boundaries, and in what circumstances, are constantly being re-negotiated.

There are four main conclusions to this chapter. First, those who work in the social services experience more violence and abuse than most other groups of workers. The British Crime Survey identified 'welfare workers' as particularly vulnerable to violence (Mayhew et al, 1989). But even among 'welfare workers', those who work in social care are more at risk, with 29% of residential workers in England and Northern Ireland and 58% of residential workers in the Scottish sample being physically attacked in the course of a year, compared with 3% of general practitioners and between 7% and 5% of nurses.

Second, it is important to recognise the vulnerability of those who work in residential services. Despite the focus in the literature on social workers, these staff actually experienced fewer physical attacks than any other job type, except home care workers. Overwhelmingly, violence and threats of violence are to be found in the residential establishments for which social services and social work departments are responsible. We can only assume that similar problems exist in the private and voluntary sectors. Most at risk are the staff who work in homes for children and young people and for those with mental health problems and severe learning difficulties. However, older people can also express violence, especially verbally, and because of their larger numbers in our survey this group was responsible for numerically the largest number of incidents recorded.

Third, violence can take many different forms, and can involve relatives as well as service users. Overall about a quarter of attacks were made by relatives of service users, rather than by service users themselves, but relatives were more likely to be the protagonists when children and young people were involved; by contrast, home care and residential workers were much more likely to be attacked by service users than by relatives. In all three samples men were more vulnerable than women to physical violence, while much abuse of black and Asian staff also involved racism (see also Chapter Six). Training programmes should help staff to understand and deal with the many different forms which violence, threats of violence and abuse can take.

Fourth, it is clear that senior managers and employers are still not providing enough help and support, despite all that has been said and written on this topic. In particular managers and staff in residential establishments were likely to feel that they received less help than necessary when the most recent incident took place. There is still much that can be done to reduce the risk of violence, to train staff to cope with violent people, and to support those who have been attacked or threatened with attack.

SIX

Discrimination at work

Barbara Davey

Introduction

This chapter explores individual and institutional discrimination in the social services. The emphasis placed on equal opportunities and anti-discriminatory practice by social services departments would lead us to expect these agencies to have an exemplary track record on this issue. With this in mind, this chapter outlines social services staff's experiences of discrimination or suspected discrimination by their employers. This is discussed in relation to difficulties involved in getting or keeping jobs because of ethnicity, gender or other grounds, including religion. Difficulties with service users and colleagues because of religious community identification in Northern Ireland are examined. The question of gender discrimination as it affects career progression is explored in Chapter Seven. Without wishing to privilege one form of discrimination over another, there is, however, a primary focus on racism not only from employers but also from service users and colleagues.

Three methodological points should be borne in mind when reading this chapter. The first concerns the first interviews which asked all questions of discrimination, racism and community identity in relation to the respondent's current job. As the length of time in their current job varied from about six months to 15 years, in addition to problems of recall, many incidents could have taken place before equal opportunities policies had a chance to make an impact. To gain a clearer picture, the same questions were asked about discrimination over the 12 months prior to second interview. Changes in discrimination over time cannot be compared because the time frames specified at each interview are different. Secondly, definitions of discrimination and racism were left to the respondents. This means there are individual variations in definitions and caution must be exercised accordingly. Thirdly, when analysing findings by ethnicity or community identity the numbers are sometimes too small to show statistical significance. Unless significance is stated, the findings should be regarded as indicative rather than conclusive.

Social services managers, social work staff, residential workers and home care staff in England, Scotland and Northern Ireland were asked at both interviews about discrimination or suspected discrimination by their employers. Only black staff in the English sample were asked about their experiences of racism from service users and their relatives and from colleagues and managers. This chapter uses the term 'black' to denote groups of staff who did not describe themselves as white. Ethnic minorities were grouped in this way because the numbers in each category were too small to enable satisfactory analysis by ethnic group. Black staff were over-sampled from staff records to ensure sufficient numbers in all job types and the data was then weighted to reflect the reported figures for the local authorities. In Northern Ireland and Scotland, staff records did not include information on ethnic background, with the result that sampling by ethnic group was not possible. No staff in the Northern Ireland sample described themselves as black or Asian and there were too few black people drawn randomly in the Scottish study to allow comparisons by ethnicity. In relation to discrimination on grounds of community identity, staff in Northern Ireland were asked at both interviews if they had experienced difficulties with service users and discrimination or harassment from colleagues or managers on the grounds of their religion. For sampling and other reasons, home care staff in Northern Ireland are not included in this chapter.

The focus of this chapter on racism is important not least because the recruitment of a social services workforce which reflects the ethnic composition of the population is an essential factor in the promotion of equal opportunities and racial equality. This includes the need to provide appropriate services to black communities and it is argued that the black population must be properly represented at all levels in social services in order to bring a black perspective on policy and practice. There is evidence that black people as service users are over-represented in the most controlling elements of social services activity and under-represented in the preventative and supportive aspects. In the mental health field, for example, people of Caribbean origin, especially young men, are over-represented in detention under the 1983 Mental Health Act, while research indicates that black people have limited access to counselling and psychotherapy (Butt and Mirza, 1996). For these and other reasons, some studies have concluded that many black users of social services "often emerge from their experience angry and alienated" (Bagley and Young, 1982, cited in Bhat et al, 1988). If social services departments are to gain the confidence of black communities, then the "visible presence of black staff and the contribution they make to the practices of the institution is likely to promote such confidence" (Roys, 1988).

Analysis of racism in the English study raises important issues for all social services departments. Although black communities generally live in areas with higher than average numbers of black people, there are few areas in the United Kingdom where there is no black or ethnic minority presence. In Scotland, people of Pakistani, Chinese and Indian origin form the largest ethnic groups at just over 1% of the total population. In the west of Scotland, there are some districts where the majority of the population is Asian (Bailey et al, 1997). In Northern Ireland although numbers are small, there are various minority ethnic groups, the largest being of Chinese origin (O'Leary, 1990).

Northern Ireland may have a smaller ethnic minority presence than England and Scotland, but it has of course the added dimension of religious community identification in employment concerns and service provision. Residential childcare provision, for example, is largely organised around the religion of the child and its parents and geopolitical boundaries can determine the accessibility of day care services (Smyth and Campbell, 1996). A number of writers have discussed the similarities between sectarianism and racism. Brewer (1991) argues that both involve social stratification and although there are differences in type and status of social marker used for categorising people into groups, both result in inequalities which operate at both institutional and individual levels of society. Both racism and sectarianism are more than simply a set of prejudiced attitudes, they embody behaviour, policies and treatment resulting in intentional and unintentional discrimination. However, one difference is that racism characterised in the classic sense by colonial exploitation and oppression can only be experienced by ethnic minorities, and although in many respects sectarianism is about Catholic disadvantage, it can be a problem for Protestants as well (Brewer, 1991).

Before looking at discrimination, this chapter will firstly outline some relevant characteristics of the workforce and distribution of the workforce by job type. Secondly, experiences of discrimination or suspected discrimination in employment are discussed for all staff in England and Scotland and for managers, social work staff and residential workers in Northern Ireland. Next the experiences of black staff in England of racism from service users, colleagues and managers are examined, followed by the experiences of discrimination on grounds of community identity for staff in Northern Ireland. Finally, the chapter outlines the views of staff of their employers' equal opportunities policies for black and Asian staff.

Characteristics of the workforce

This section outlines characteristics of the workforce in terms of gender in the three studies, ethnicity in England and community identity in Northern Ireland.

Gender

Within the personal social services, women comprise a majority of the workforce. In England, this was 86% for both black and white staff. In Scotland, women formed nearly 90% of the workforce and in Northern Ireland this figure was nearly 95%, where more than three quarters of managers, social workers and residential workers and all home care workers were women.

Ethnicity in the England sample

Fifteen per cent of staff in four of the five local authorities in the English panel classified themselves as black or belonging to other minority 'ethnic' groups. Authority C, a county council had a negligible number of black staff and is excluded from the profile.

In its 1992 study of 41 local authorities, the Commission for Racial Equality (CRE) found only one in three had demonstrably achieved a workforce that reflected the local ethnic minority working population (CRE, 1995). Figure 6.1 shows the ethnic composition of the social services workforce in the four local authorities compared with the population of working age and suggests a variation between 10% and 35% of black and Asian groups in the four local authorities. Black staff were under-represented in the outer London authority A, slightly over-represented in the metropolitan district B, and greatly over-represented in the inner London Authority E. Some of the variation here is possibly a reflection of employment practices and implementation of equal opportunities policies, although of course the issue of representation is more complex than this. Measures are likely to vary according to specific ethnic group, gender, age and job type (see Balloch *et al*, 1996, pp 104-5 for more detailed discussion).

Figure 6.1: Representation of black staff in social services: percentages of black residents of working age in each local authority in the survey and in the NISW sample

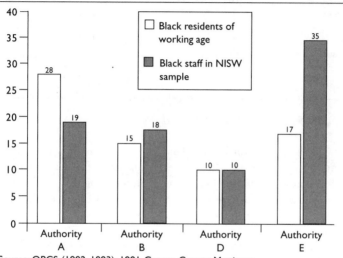

Source: OPCS (1992; 1993); 1991 Census County Monitors

Table 6.1 shows the sample of black workers at first and second interviews. Almost 8 out of 10 black staff classified themselves as black Caribbean, black African or black other. Less than one in seven belonged to Indian, Pakistani or Bangladeshi ethnic groups. Almost 9 in 10 were either born in the UK or had lived here for more than 20 years. The minority ethnic population age structure has a younger profile with a relatively large proportion of black and some Asian populations in the younger working ages 25-44 (Haskey, 1996). In the English sample, black social work staff and home care workers were significantly younger than white colleagues. For social work staff, the mean age for black staff was 37 years compared to 42 years for white staff and for home care workers, the mean age for black staff was 42 years compared to 46 years for white staff. Overall, nearly half of all black staff were aged under 40 compared with less than one third of white staff. There was some variation between the four local authorities, again possibly reflecting a variation in implementation of equal opportunities policies of the authorities in our sample.

Table 6.1: Ethnic group of black staff in the English sample: percentages at first interview and second interview

Ethnicity	First interview	Second interview
Black Caribbean	63	69
Black African	10	5
Black Other	7	6
Indian	10	9
Pakistani	3	4
Bangladeshi	<1	<1
Other group	7	7
n	213	137

Community identity in Northern Ireland

At first interview, the Northern Ireland sample was asked with which community they identified. Brewer (1991) maintains that Catholics are not under-represented in the social work profession and that most social work students trained each year are now Catholic. In our sample 45% described themselves as Catholic, 33% as Protestant, 19% as 'Neither' and 1% as 'Other'. In the Northern Ireland Census 1991, 38% described themselves as Catholic, 43% Presbyterian, Church of Ireland or Methodist and 8% other. Seven per cent did not answer the question and 4% of the population said they had no religion (DoH and Social Services Registrar General Northern Ireland, 1992). The much higher figure of 19% in our sample who said 'Neither' may be explained by answers from those who reject affiliations based on religion, or who consciously reject or feel uncomfortable with applying such categorisations to themselves or having them applied by others. There were considerable differences between those aged under 40 and over 40 in the community identification of those in the manager and social work staff groups. Nearly two thirds of managers and more than half of social work staff aged under 40 described their identification as Catholic compared with one third of managers and social workers aged over 40. Although there are differences in age distribution between Catholic and Protestant populations with the Catholic community having a younger age profile, this could also suggest à change in recruitment patterns in recent years (SACHR, 1987; McConkey, 1995). As Brewer (1991) points out, social work is now seen as a means of Catholic social mobility.

Current job

The following shows the distribution of the workforce by ethnicity and gender in the English sample and by community identification and gender in Northern Ireland.

England

Black staff were more likely to be field social work staff or residential workers than managers or home care workers. Table 6.2 shows percentages of black and white women and men in five job categories at first interview.

Table 6.2: Job type: percentages by ethnicity and gender at first interview

Job type	All	Black women	White women	Black men	White men	Black staff	White Staff
Manager	10	5	8	11	29	6	11
Social work staff	14	17	12	21	22	17	13
Home care	40	29	48	11	9	26	43
Residential	29	42	26	44	30	43	27
Social work assistant/ other social care	7	7	6	13	10	8	6
% of whole sample	100	13	73	2	12	15	85

Some studies have shown that black workers in social services are often valued for their 'expertise' in cultural and racial issues rather than their expertise generally (Butt et al, 1994; Butt, 1994). This can have consequences for career progression and at first interview, more than six out of 10 black staff agreed with the statement 'Black and Asian workers have to be very much better than white workers to make the same progress in their careers'. Overall, black staff were significantly more dissatisfied than white staff with their career progress (Balloch et al, 1995). Table 6.2 shows the under-representation of black staff in management at first interview. By the second interview, 3% of our sample had been promoted from non-management to management positions. Although proportionately fewer black than white staff had been promoted, the difference could not be tested for reliability owing to the small numbers involved. Although black staff showed particular interest in training leading to better qualifications and were more likely than white staff to undertake training which involved self-study, there was no evidence of progress in recruiting more black managers by promotion.

Northern Ireland

Table 6.3: Community identification: percentages by job type and gender

Community identified with:	All	Manager		Social work staff		Residential worker	
		Women	Men	Women	Men	Women	Men
Catholic	45	46	42	43	55	47	39
Protestant	33	35	38	35	18	32	51
Neither	19	17	20	17	27	19	0
Other	1	0	0	2	0	0	10

Table 6.3 shows that community identity did not generally influence job type for either women or men in social services in Northern Ireland. The exceptions were the smaller percentage of men social work staff and a larger percentage of men residential workers who described themselves as Protestant. A higher percentage of men social work staff said they identified with neither community.

Discrimination by employers

Discussion of employment patterns typically revolves around whether they are structured by discrimination or disadvantage. Disadvantage arguments describe situations where individuals, by their membership of a particular group, are subject to unequal life chances. For example, women's caring roles within the family result in periods of part-time working and career breaks which then impact on occupational mobility. Discrimination arguments focus on barriers in the workplace where individuals are subject to discrimination by an organisational culture in which equal opportunities are subverted. The questions in the survey were concerned with staff's perceptions of discrimination by employers in relation to getting and keeping jobs, on race, gender, disability, sexual orientation or other grounds. Before discussing racial discrimination, this section will examine staff's experiences of all forms of discrimination.

At first interview, 16% of staff in England, 12% of staff in Scotland and 14% of staff in Northern Ireland said they had experienced discrimination in one form or another by employers in their current job. The most common reason given by staff in all three countries for the most recent incident of discrimination was gender but many staff selected more than one form of discrimination. Unexpectedly, proportionately more men than women complained on grounds of gender in all three studies. Job type was a main indicator of those likely to believe they had been a victim of discrimination, especially field social work staff. As would be expected, in England black staff in all job types were significantly more likely to have experienced discrimination than white staff. The percentages of those believing they had been subject to some form of discrimination might appear high for a profession which works within an anti-discriminatory framework but many of these incidents had happened a number of years prior to first interview. A more relevant picture might be gained from looking at these experiences in the 12 months prior to the second interview with staff who remained in the sample.

Eight per cent of staff in England said they had experienced discrimination within 12 months of the second interview, but there were less than 4% in Scotland and a similar figure in Northern Ireland. Although numbers are small, the most common reason for the most recent incident given in both Northern Ireland and Scotland was religion, followed by gender. In England gender was the most common reason given, for both black and white staff, followed by race. There were negligible numbers giving grounds of disability or sexual orientation for their most recent experience of discrimination. Many staff selected more than one reason for discrimination and because of this and the small numbers for many of the grounds, for example sexual orientation analysis was focused on whether or not *any* form of discrimination had been experienced.

In all three studies, in a similar pattern to the findings at first interview, there were again proportionately more men than women complaining of discrimination, in Northern Ireland and Scotland significantly so. In England, this applied to both black and white staff. There were also variations between job types. In Scotland, proportionately more field social work staff said they had experienced discrimination than other job types, especially men. Men residential workers were also more likely than their women colleagues to report a discriminatory incident in the previous twelve months. In Northern Ireland, there was little variation between job types but more men than women social work staff complained.

In England, analysis by gender, ethnicity and job type shows that social work staff, followed by managers were most likely to say they had experienced discrimination. In our sample, more men social work staff and residential workers complained of discrimination than women in these job types. The fact that proportionately more social work staff and particularly men reported discrimination, especially on grounds of gender, needs to be explored further.

Racial discrimination by employers

The facts of racial discrimination in recruitment are well known. Various Policy Studies Institute (PSI) reports have shown that both Afro-Caribbean and Asian people are less likely to be appointed to a range of jobs than similarly qualified white applicants (Brown and Gay, 1986). In a study of nursing in the NHS, most staff believed that racial discrimination in recruitment existed in the NHS and 26% of both black and Asian nursing staff believed they had been refused jobs in the NHS for ethnic reasons (Beishon et al, 1995). In the English Workforce studies, 10% of black staff reported that they had experienced or suspected racial discrimination in relation to getting or keeping particular jobs within the 12 months prior to second interview, compared with less than 1% of white staff. Although numbers were small, proportionately twice as many men as women reported racial discrimination, a gender pattern similar to that for other forms of discrimination. However, 3% of black women believed they had experienced discrimination on grounds of gender as well as race.

Analysis of the most recent incidents suggested that most occurred during daily work routines rather than job applications and there were complaints of racial discrimination in all four authorities. The confidence to initiate grievance procedures is important to the success of equal opportunities policies. Research has indicated that the formalisation of procedures alone is not enough and that commitment of senior management to the principles of equal opportunities within organisations is essential (Mason and Jewson, 1992). Black staff in our sample were generally aware of grievance procedures, but in spite of this only half of those who had experienced racial discrimination had made a formal protest about the most recent incident. Those who had not complained formally either thought a protest would not be worth making or that it might damage their future prospects.

Racism from service users and colleagues

Some indication of the problem of racial abuse at work has been obtained by the 1988 British Crime Survey (Mayhew et al, 1993). In that study, respondents were asked whether they had been subjected to verbal abuse from someone they came into contact with in their job, other than a colleague, in the last 14 months. One in seven people, almost equal proportions of black and white people, had been verbally abused during that period. However, of black and Asian people who had been verbally abused, approximately half attributed a racial motive to the abuse, compared with 2% white staff (Aye Maung and Mirrlees-Black, 1994). The Workforce studies in England also showed that there was no difference between black and white staff in the extent to which they were subjected to physical attacks, threats of violence or verbal abuse by service users or their relatives but only black and Asian staff were asked about racism (see Chapter Five for a discussion on violence). At both interviews, black and Asian staff were asked about their experiences of racism from service users and colleagues. At second interview, staff were asked about the most recent incident, when and where it had happened, a profile of the perpetrator and how the racism had been expressed. This section examines these experiences, how staff were affected by these incidents and the level of support available to them from their departments.

Racism from service users and relatives

In the PSI study of nursing in the NHS, 66% of black and 58% of Asian nursing staff reported difficulties, hostilities or aggression from patients to do with race, compared with 12% white staff (Beishon et al, 1995). In our first interview, 75% of black and Asian respondents said they experienced racism from service users or their relatives, in their current job. One in six black or Asian staff said this happened 'fairly often' or 'very often'. This varied significantly by local authority with more than 8 out of 10 black staff reporting an experience of racism in the inner London borough and less than six out of ten in the outer London borough. Some of these incidents had occurred some years previously and to get a more up-to-date picture it is more relevant to locate incidents in the twelve months before the second interview.

Of the remaining panel, 41% of black and Asian staff said they had experienced racism from service users or relatives in the 12 months before second interview. One in 8 staff said this happened 'very often' or 'fairly often'. Analysis of the most recent incidents showed that the majority of the 59 cases involved a service user rather than a relative, a quarter of whom were children or adolescents, a fifth adults with learning difficulties, physical disabilities or mental health problems and two fifths older people. These figures are not intended to identify any particular user group as they are partly a reflection of the representation of particular groups of staff in the sample. Nearly all the perpetrators were white, both women and men, although the majority of those at the receiving end were women because of the gender composition of the workforce. Most incidents took place in the day time, two thirds somewhere in the staff member's workplace and the others in the service user's home. Preliminary analysis suggests that most concerned racist abuse, racist swear words, insults or comments. Other examples included service users inappropriately questioning the authority of the respondents, not wanting to be touched by the respondent or asking to be dealt with by a white person. Although this may give us a picture of a typical range of incidents, it does not tell us the frequency with which such racism takes place. We can examine however, who is experiencing these incidents. Analysis was undertaken on whether or not racism had been experienced in relation to gender, job type, authority and age differences. The main predictor was job type with social work staff significantly more likely to say they had experienced racism within twelve months of second interview than the average for all job types (Butt and Davey, 1997).

Racism from colleagues and managers

In NHS nursing, Beishon et al (1995) found that 37% of black and Asian nursing staff indicated difficulties with colleagues for ethnic reasons, a lower incidence than difficulties with patients. Similarly, in the Workforce studies at first interview, fewer black staff said they experienced racism from colleagues and managers than from service users in their current job. However, the proportion, 45%, was still very high and one in 14 of all black staff said they experienced racism from this source 'fairly often' or 'very often'. Social workers and social work assistants were significantly more likely to say they had experienced this form of racism than the other job types. As before, many incidents had occurred some years previously and a more accurate current picture may be gained from a time period of 12 months before second interview.

At second interview, of the remaining respondents, 27% of black and Asian staff said they experienced racism from colleagues or managers within 12 months prior to interview. One in 12 said this happened 'fairly often' or 'very often'. Analysis of the 41 most recent incidents showed that nearly all took place in the daytime somewhere in the staff member's workplace. All but one said the perpetrator was white with 62% women compared with 38% men identified as responsible for the 'most recent' incident, an over-representation of men as they form less than 15% of the workforce. In half of cases, another person was present at the time of the incident, mainly other colleagues or workers. Almost three quarters had experienced this from a colleague rather than a manager and more than half, from a colleague on the same work/team. This is particularly important since it means challenging racism also implies challenging team dynamics. Fifteen per cent said their own line manager had been responsible for the incident. Preliminary analysis suggests that the most frequent complaints concerned racist swear words, insults or other comments followed by complaints mainly from social work staff, where the authority of the respondent was inappropriately questioned. A small number concerned the general attitude of manager and/or colleagues. Similarly to the question of racism from service users, this gives a picture of a typical range of incidents, although not the frequency. To identify who was experiencing this kind of racism, further analysis was undertaken on whether or not racism from colleagues or managers had been experienced in the previous twelve months by gender, job type, authority and age. The results showed a similar pattern both to those reporting racism in their current job at first interview and those experiencing racism from service users (Butt and Davey, 1997). The main predictor was job type with social work staff and to a lesser extent managers, significantly more likely to say they had experienced racism from colleagues and managers than the average for all job types.

Effects of racism and help available in dealing with racism

Although many studies do not include examination of 'low level' racial harassment, the potentially damaging nature of racial abuse and other types of racially motivated insults has been discussed (Virdee, 1995). It is likely that many staff were emotionally affected in some way by these incidents, especially when perpetrated by colleagues and managers. Analysis of stress scores at first interview measured by GHQ12 showed that the mean scores for those who had experienced racism from colleagues or managers in their current job was 3.10, significantly higher than the average for those staff who had not, 1.50. This finding remained true when other key variables, job type, gender, age and physical health were taken into account (see Balloch et al, 1995, Chapter Six for further discussion). At second interview, 75% said they were affected by the last incident of racism from a service user, one in three 'quite a lot' or 'very much', these figures rising to 80%, with two out of three 'quite a lot' or 'very much' affected when the perpetrator was a colleague or manager.

Departments should have clear policies for supporting staff in these issues and staff should be confident that they will gain the support they need from their department. At first interview, all black and Asian staff were asked their views of the help available to them in dealing with racism. Table 6.4 shows a degree of uncertainty on the part of black staff about whether clear policies existed in their department and just under half knew positively that such policies existed. In spite of this, 62% black and Asian staff were confident in the level of support available from their department in the event of racism from service users. The data suggest this trust was misplaced, as the majority of those who had expressed confidence said they had not received the help they needed for their most recent experience. Confident or not, only four out of ten felt they had been given the right amount of help from their department. Ten per cent, all home care and residential workers, said no help had been available and a minority had not asked for help.

Table 6.4 shows that only half of all black staff expressed confidence that they would get support from their department in dealing with racism from co-workers and managers. Three quarters of staff who had this experience in the 12 months before second interview said that the help available to them was less or a lot less than they needed.

The data suggest that black staff have to look beyond formal structures for support in dealing with racism. When asked what helped them most, the common sources of support were other work colleagues, followed by friends and then family.

Table 6.4: Views about support in dealing with racism at first interview: percentages of black staff

Aspect of support		All black staff %
Is there a clear policy in your department for supporting staff who experience racism from clients and relatives?		
	yes	45
	no	20
	can't say	36
Suppose you were faced with racism from clients and their relatives, how confident are you that you would get the support you needed from the department?		
	very/fairly	62
	not very/ not at all	38
Is there a clear policy in your department for supporting staff who experience racism from co-workers and managers?		
	yes	46
	no	18
	can't say	36
Supposing you were faced with racism from co-workers and managers, how confident are you that you would get the support you needed from the department?		
	Very/fairly	50
	not very/ not at all	50

Discrimination by service users and colleagues on grounds of community identity

Some similarities between racism and sectarianism were outlined earlier, but unlike racism (which can only be experienced by ethnic minorities), discrimination on grounds of community identity can affect Protestants as well as Catholics. Another difference, as Brewer (1991) points out, is that religion is not based on perceptual cues and may be discarded or avoided, as 19% of our sample did, although stereotypical cues such as names and variations in pronunciation may operate in a similar manner. In both interviews, managers, social work staff and residential workers in Northern Ireland were asked if there had been difficulties with service users or if clients had refused a service from them on grounds of perceived community identity or whether they had experienced discrimination or harassment from colleagues or managers for the same reason. This section examines these experiences as well as the effects on staff and the help available from employers.

Discrimination from service users

At first interview, 12% of managers, social work staff and residential workers said that in their current job users had refused a service from them on grounds of perceived community identity but that this was a rare or infrequent occurrence. Twenty-eight per cent said there had been difficulties for them in working with users on these grounds but again this was infrequent or rare. There was an indication that social work staff were more likely to say they had experienced difficulties than managers or residential workers but this was not statistically significant. Although it might be expected that there would be geographical differences, there was little variation across the four Boards (McConkey, 1995). When the staff remaining in the study were asked about refusal of service in the 12 months before second interview, the vast majority, more than 8 in 10 in Catholic, Protestant and 'Neither' groups said this had never happened to them. Where there had been refusal of service this was described as a rare or infrequent occurrence by 12% Catholics, 10% 'Neither' and only 2% Protestants. In relation to difficulties with service users, again staff said this had happened from time to time or rarely although the differences between Catholic and Protestant were more marked. Twenty-one per cent of Catholics, 16% 'Neither' and 3% Protestant said it had been difficult to work with users because of the staff member's perceived community identity (McConkey et al, 1997).

Discrimination from colleagues and managers

At first interview, only a small minority of respondents, around 3% overall, reported that they had experienced discrimination, intimidation or harassment from colleagues or managers in their current job. Protestant workers in all three job types appeared to be slightly less likely to feel they had been discriminated against by colleagues or managers and again there was very little variation between the four Boards (McConkey, 1995). At second interview, the likelihood of Catholic workers and those describing themselves as 'Neither' or 'Other' reporting discrimination, intimidation or harassment from colleagues or managers in the previous 12 months was slightly higher than for Protestant staff, although the vast majority in all groups said this had never happened to them. Five per cent of Catholics and 6% of those self-classifying as 'Neither' had experienced this from time to time or rarely in the previous 12 months and 2% of the 'Neither' group said this happened fairly often. These differences did not reach statistical significance (McConkey et al, 1997).

Effects and help available in dealing with discrimination

As in the experiences of racism, it would be expected that difficulties with service users on grounds of perceived community identity or experience of discrimination from colleagues and managers would have affected staff in some way and maybe also had an impact on job satisfaction. The association between job satisfaction and stress as measured by GHQ12 is explored in Chapter 4. Here the mean summed job satisfaction scores and mean stress scores as measured by GHQ12 were compared for those who had and those who had not experienced discrimination from service users and others in the previous year. Table 6.5 shows that for Catholic workers and those who described themselves as 'Neither', there are indications that mean job satisfaction scores were lower in the presence of discriminatory behaviour by users and others. For Protestant workers, whose summed satisfaction scores appeared to be higher overall, there does not appear to be an association between discrimination and lower job satisfaction.

Table 6.5 suggests that for Catholics and 'Neither' groups the experience of discrimination was associated with higher stress, reaching statistical significance for the 'Neither' group. This was not the case for Protestant workers.

The clarity and communication of policies and the availability of organisational support for staff exposed to discrimination on grounds of perceived community identity are similar issues to those discussed in relation to racism. There was less uncertainty about policies among staff in Northern Ireland than among black staff in England. The majority of managers, social work staff and residential workers said their employers had clear 'fair employment' policies to support staff who experienced discrimination from colleagues and managers, although 21% did not know if they did. Although numbers were small, the data suggest greater satisfaction among staff in Northern Ireland with the level of organisational help available for dealing with discrimination than among black and Asian staff in the English sample. In Northern Ireland, only 14% said that the amount of help available was less than necessary (McConkey et al, 1997).

Table 6.5: Satisfaction and stress: mean scores by community identity

Community Identity	Mean summed satisfaction scores		Mean GHQ12 scores	
	Experienced discrimination	Had not experienced discrimination	Experienced discrimination	Had not experienced discrimination
Catholic	66.43	70.77	3.18	1.93
Protestant	77.75	73.66	1.07	2.19
Neither	63.76	69.89	4.16*	2.14

*$p<=0.05$

Equal opportunities policies for black and Asian staff

Despite some criticism, it is generally agreed that equal opportunities policies (EOPs) are important in effecting change in both employment and service provision. The 1988 CRE survey of social services departments found that those departments which had equal opportunities policies in employment were more likely to have considered these measures in service provision (CRE, 1989). One way of assessing the effectiveness of a department's policy is through ethnic record keeping and monitoring (ERKM) systems, yet these are not commonplace (Butt et al, 1994). In the absence of statistical evidence as to how equal opportunities policies for black and Asian staff are working, this section examines staff's perceptions of the importance placed by their employers on this issue and their views on any progress being made and improvements needed.

All staff in England, Northern Ireland and Scotland were asked at first interview how much importance their department placed on equal opportunities in recruitment, promotion and training for black and Asian staff. There were significant differences between the perceptions of black and white staff in the English sample on this issue with 65% of black staff feeling that too little importance was given to these questions, compared with 20% white staff. Black social work staff and managers were significantly more likely than other job types to feel their department placed too little importance on equal opportunities, except in metropolitan authority D. Slightly more than half of staff in Northern Ireland and Scotland felt that their employers placed the right amount of importance on equal opportunities, similar proportions to white staff in England. When asked what progress was being made in this area, there was a degree of uncertainty on this issue in the English authorities with 35% black staff and 44% white staff unsure. Black staff were more pessimistic than white staff with 22% of black staff but only 8% of white staff saying their department was not making progress. Generally, this was not considered an area of concern in Northern Ireland where more than three quarters of managers, social work staff and residential workers either did not know or thought the question was not applicable. In Scotland more than half did not know. Staff in metropolitan authority D were also significantly more likely to be optimistic about progress being made on this issue.

At second interview, staff in the three studies were asked how they would improve equal opportunities in their authority. Although this question resulted in many diverse suggestions, the most common response from staff in Scotland and Northern Ireland was to the effect that equal opportunities policies were working quite well. Only 5% of responses in Scotland and 6% of responses in Northern Ireland suggested giving higher priority to the issue of equal opportunities. In England, around two thirds of the panel responded to this question. Of these, 37% of black staff compared with 13% of white staff said they wanted higher priority given to equal opportunities. Verbatim comments from black staff in all four authorities expressed concern that equal opportunities were not being implemented and at the lack of evidence that policies were being put into practice. As one manager commented: "it's time that the policies adopted are actually adhered to in practice". A social worker said: "I would like to see more positive monitoring of the policy".

Conclusions

In drawing out conclusions from the three studies, two points of caution need to be made. First, some of the statistics presented are based on small numbers and therefore any conclusions based on them must be treated accordingly. Second, the definitions of discrimination and racism in the studies were subjective and preliminary analysis indicates that the meanings and values represented by the responses can vary considerably, as indeed is the case with any subjective measure. Further work is needed in this area.

Nevertheless, these findings do provide important insights into the experiences of staff in the social services. Although opinions differ as to whether increased numbers of black workers in social services are a sign of the success of equal opportunities policies, it is generally accepted that black workers are more prominent in social services in England (Butt et al, 1994; Butt, 1994). Although the issue of ethnic representation is a complex one, our evidence does emphasise the under-representation of black staff at management level. Furthermore, black staff were less satisfied with their career progress than white staff, yet there is evidence that black staff were particularly interested in training leading to better qualifications and more likely to undertake training involving self-study (see Chapter Eight). It is reasonable to think that this is part of an attempt to become more mobile in their careers and supporting their aspirations for training would be a way of helping develop more black managers. Overall black staff were more likely than white staff to feel that their department put insufficient effort into implementing equal opportunities in recruitment, promotion and training and were uncertain or pessimistic about progress in these areas. Authorities might examine the commitment of their senior management to equal opportunities, since research has shown this is essential to their success (Mason and Jewson, 1992). Training might provide one avenue for improvement and our evidence is that, where authorities offered management courses, two thirds of participants reported that their understanding of equal opportunities policies had improved (see Chapter Eight).

Even in local authorities and job types where representativeness was not such a substantive issue, this has not meant that black staff no longer experience racism from their colleagues. One in 12 black staff said they had experienced racism 'fairly often' or 'very often' in the twelve months before second interview. Further analysis is needed to explore the working situations of these staff. The English study further suggests that black workers continue to experience abuse by service users and their relatives. The fact that significantly more social work staff than other job types said they had experienced racism from these sources points to the possibility of a greater awareness of anti-discriminatory practice among these staff. Of concern too is that black workers felt that departments were not providing adequate support to them in these circumstances. Local authorities have little control over the expression of racism by service users (although they can make explicit their opposition to racism). They do, however, have substantial control over the expression of racism by their employees, and over the support services to those experiencing racist abuse from whatever source, and it is in these areas that, in the views of black staff, local authorities were failing. Although all authorities in our survey had equal opportunities policies, their implementation had apparently failed to ensure that all staff were sufficiently aware of the policy and its implications.

In Northern Ireland, discrimination or difficulties with service users or colleagues and managers on the grounds of community identity was generally a rare or infrequent occurrence. Where discrimination was present, however, there were suggestions of an association with lower job satisfaction and higher stress scores for Catholic workers and especially for those who described themselves as belonging to neither community. Most staff in Northern Ireland were aware of their employers 'fair employment' policies and where staff had sought help for dealing with discrimination, the majority were satisfied with the amount of help available.

In relation to discrimination by employers, in England, Scotland and Northern Ireland, the data suggest a pattern where more men than women and, in general, social work staff more than other job types made complaints of discrimination by their employers, including discrimination on grounds of gender. These results point to the need for further work to examine the experiences of men as a gender minority in social services, and the possibility that a greater awareness of and training in equal opportunities among social work staff is associated with a greater readiness to classify experiences as discrimination.

Discrimination clearly remains an issue for many social services staff. The experience of discrimination, especially from colleagues or from managers and the lack of support available to deal with such experiences, requires employers to take appropriate steps to gain the confidence of staff that they can make good their claims to provide an anti-discriminatory environment for their work.

SEVEN

Gender and career progression

Jay Ginn and Mike Fisher

Introduction

A key element of any human resources strategy is to utilise to the full the capacities of the workforce in the service of the organisation. The question of human potential has a particular resonance in social care agencies, whose purpose is to maximise the life chances of service users (or at least to minimise the impact of adverse circumstances). Social care agencies also work within an anti-discriminatory framework, intended to challenge the role of prejudice and discrimination in compounding disadvantage. On all these counts, therefore, we might expect some consistency between the egalitarian and humanistic values of social care agencies and practice with their own staff. As we have shown in Chapter Six, however, discriminatory processes within social services often mirror those in wider society.

This chapter will explore whether discrimination plays a role in women's career progression in social services. The immediate reason to ask this question is that although women comprised between 86% and 95% of the workforces studied, the proportion of managers who were women ranged from 60% to 71% (Table 7.1).

Table 7.1: Percentages of all staff and managerial staff who were women

	All staff	Managers
England	86	65
Scotland	90	60
Northern Ireland	95	71

The more senior the management position, the less frequently it was occupied by women. The Social Services Inspectorate reported in 1991 that 12% of directors of social services departments were women and 18% of senior managers (SSI, 1991). Despite the creation of many more English authorities by 1997, the proportion of women directors remained the same, although the proportion of authorities with no senior women managers had decreased from 31% to 18% (SSI, 1997) Across the UK as a whole in 1997, there were 192 social services authorities, of which 39 (20%) were directed by women. In Scotland, there were nine women among 32 directors, in Northern Ireland one of four, and in Wales one of 22. In England, London boroughs had the highest proportion (33%), followed by metropolitan and unitary authorities (19%) and counties (16%).

Seniority and career progression

In our studies of the workforce, we aimed to explore the influence of gender on occupational attainment. Our concerns included but were much broader than whether women entered the occupational category we had called manager. We therefore introduced the concept of 'seniority', intentionally defining it more broadly than the concept of manager. 'Senior' included, for example, senior social workers, and team leaders in social work, home care organisers and managers, and officers in charge and managers in residential establishments (for full details, see Ginn et al, 1997)

Table 7.2 shows the proportion of women and men in each occupational category at first interview who had attained seniority as defined above. In this analysis, where we wish to know the proportions of senior staff within each of the occupational categories of field social work, home care and residential work, we include managers in their respective occupational category (for example, home care organisers are included in home care). There is, however, another kind of manager – central and strategic managers with responsibility for planning and managing the agency as a whole rather than within any one occupational group: membership of this category of manager would represent promotion from *any* other job type, and so we include throughout this chapter a separate column showing this group as a percentage of *all* staff. Home care staff in Northern Ireland are not included in this chapter for sampling and other reasons (see discussion in Chapter One).

Table 7.2 : Percentages of staff who were senior by occupational category and gender

	Field social work		Home care		Residential		Central	
	Women	Men	Women	Men	Women	Men	Women	Men
England	21	38	4	16	7	16	1	8
Scotland	12	31	3	23	3	8	1	8
Northern Ireland	20	41	–	–	10	34	4	20

In each job type, a smaller proportion of women than men occupied senior posts. For example, 12% of women but 31% of men field social work staff were senior in Scotland. This implies that there are gender-specific factors influencing women's career progression, which is the subject of the rest of this chapter.

The concept of vertical sex segregation

The disproportionate representation of men in senior positions in the career structure, and of women in lower positions, is usually referred to as vertical sex segregation, and is a characteristic of most occupations. For example, in studies summarised by Evetts (1994a) it characterises medicine, law, teaching, the civil service, the NHS workforce generally and nursing in particular, banking, pharmacy, dentistry, accountancy, and scientific and engineering occupations.

The studies of the NHS workforce are particularly relevant as they also concern a public sector 'caring' profession, traditionally offering employment and careers to women (Alimo-Metcalfe, 1991; Equal Opportunities Commission, 1991; Seccombe et al, 1993). Seccombe et al (1993) show that men comprise 12% of community nurse managers, 14% of hospital nurse managers and 37% of nursing officer posts, a disproportionate share given that they were 7% of the nursing workforce. Women took longer to reach nursing officer posts (18 years versus eight for men), and even those who did not have a career break took 14 years (Davies and Rosser, 1986).

Explanations of vertical sex segregation in nursing have emphasised the role of part-time working and career breaks. Part-time status is associated with nurses in lower grades, who show more dissatisfaction with career opportunities than full-time staff (Seccombe et al, 1993).

There was a link between career progression and career breaks to have children or for other reasons: of the third of women who had taken at least one such break, 11% lost seniority on return, a pattern echoed in Dex's analysis of women's occupational mobility (Dex, 1987). They were also less likely to occupy senior posts in comparison with colleagues with the same length of service. Jackson and Barber (1993) confirm that senior women were less likely than their junior colleagues to have taken a career break, and add that women's access to training was adversely affected by their family responsibilities. A study in local government in Scotland also showed that women promoted before a career break often returned to a basic grade post because there were no senior posts available or not available part-time (McDonald et al,1990).

The analysis of the role of career breaks raises the question of how career is defined, and whether it recognises the experiences of women (Crompton and Sanderson, 1986; Coyle, 1988; Evetts, 1994b). The concept that a career comprises full-time, continuous work, with progressive upward mobility, more closely characterises the careers of men than women, and the expectation that women's careers should be similar contributes to what Davies and Rosser describe as a "climate hostile to women" in the NHS (Davies and Rosser, 1986, p 59). This pattern of defining men's careers as the norm has also been analysed in a study of local government, where it combined with the perception that women age earlier than men (Itzin and Phillipson, 1993).

Similar work has been undertaken in social services and specifically social work (Hallett, 1990; Grimwood and Popplestone, 1993; Taylor, 1994). Grimwood and Popplestone draw particular attention to the question of whether the front-line task of caring is perceived as a distinct role for women, while managing, especially its controlling aspect, is seen as 'men's work'. Hallett emphasises the limitations that family commitments can place on career advancement, and explores the relationship between the natural capacity to care and the discrete, technical skills required to justify specialisation and higher rewards. Baines echoes this analysis and underlines that in order to underpin its professionalisation, caring has been redefined by men in terms of technical expertise (Baines, 1991). Murray has recently explored the relevance of different theories of vertical sex segregation to social work, and concluded that several of the traditional theories did not apply (Murray, 1997). Women social workers did not suffer from a lack of educational qualifications, low job stability, or low trade union membership, while other explanations, such as family responsibilities, lack of workplace training, and discrimination remained potent factors. Crucially, the claim that women might have lower aspirations for promotion was not supported by her earlier study showing no significant differences between women and men social work students' career orientations (Taylor, 1994).

The question of aspirations is vital if we are to change women's under-representation in management and to defend expenditure on training for women. A view commonly held by male managers is that women are insufficiently committed to work to merit senior positions (Schein et al, 1996; Wacjman, 1996). Hakim has argued that, in addressing the issue of women's under-representation, we have ignored a group of women who prefer paid work to take second place to family and home (Hakim, 1995). She reviews survey data showing that women are less committed than men to paid work, and concludes that there are two groups of women, "fairly evenly balanced in size: a group giving priority to marriage and child-rearing as their central life activity, and another group giving priority to market work as their central life activity" (p 405). This conclusion is contested by other researchers, who argue that it is lack of good quality, affordable childcare facilities, rather than lack of work commitment, which underlies women's 'preference' for part-time employment (Ginn, 1996; Ginn et al, 1996; Ginn and Sandell, 1997). Commitment to family life does not inevitably rule out commitment to work, as Warren shows in her study of women home helps, who were highly committed to the quality of their service, despite prioritising responsibilities to their family (Warren, 1990).

This account has shown the widespread nature of vertical segregation in the labour market, and its prevalence in the workforce of social services agencies. Part-time working and career breaks, mainly for family reasons, strongly influence women's career progress, in a context where caring is often seen as women's strength while the control function of managers is seen primarily as the preserve of men. Although it has been argued that women have lower aspirations towards seniority, the evidence suggests that this underestimates the different effects of the tension between work and home on women and men, and does not in any case apply to the aspirations of women social workers. We now turn to the evidence from the Workforce studies.

Attaining seniority in social services

As might be expected, seniority as defined above was strongly associated with age (Table 7.3; see also Chapter Two). For example, in England 22%

of field social work staff in their thirties were senior, compared with 31% in their forties. In general, staff were rarely in senior positions under the age of 30, and about a third of senior field social work staff were aged between 40-49. In home care, there was, however, no association between age and seniority.

Table 7.3: Percentages of staff in each occupational category who were senior, by age

Age	Field social work	Home care	Residential	Central
Under 30				
England	6	4	1	0
Scotland	10	0	0	0
Northern Ireland	0	–	0	0
30-39				
England	22	4	15	3
Scotland	10	7	5	1
Northern Ireland	26	–	12	6
40-49				
England	31	5	13	3
Scotland	36	1	10	3
Northern Ireland	30	–	20	14
Over 50				
England	28	4	5	1
Scotland	17	3	1	0
Northern Ireland	29	–	16	8

Fewer staff under 30 occupied senior field social work posts in Northern Ireland than in England or Scotland. The proportion of residential staff in senior positions was consistently low in Scotland relative to other occupational groups or other samples suggesting a poor career structure and development for these staff. Detailed analysis of the English sample showed that women were older than men when promoted to a senior post, irrespective of occupational category. The mean ages at promotion for women and men were 39 and 35 in field social work, 36 and 33 in residential work, and 37 and 33 in central/strategic staff.

Longer service in social care allows experience in a wider range of jobs, and this in turn is associated with seniority, particularly among field social work staff. Among these staff with four or more jobs, 38% held senior posts in England, 19% in Scotland and 35% in Northern Ireland, while the percentages for staff with two or fewer jobs were much lower 22%, 14% and 8%.

A similar picture was evident for educational and professional qualifications. Within each job type, seniority was closely related to the level of the highest educational qualification possessed, suggesting that a lower level of educational qualification plays a part in limiting women's career progression. Northern Ireland was an exception to this pattern: the influence of educational level was restricted to attaining senior posts in the central/strategic staff group, perhaps reflecting the equally important role of qualifications in seniority and the generally higher levels of qualification among Northern Ireland staff.

Except in home care, where possession of such qualifications was rare, professional qualifications were associated with seniority in each occupational category. In the English study, for example, a third of field social work staff with a professional social work qualification held senior positions, compared with only 9% of those without a professional qualification. In Scotland the figures were a quarter compared with 5%, and in Northern Ireland a third compared with 3%. As shown in Chapter Two, women had lower levels of education and professional qualifications than men. However, this did not fully explain their lower occupational attainment. Looking more closely at a sub-group of staff in the English study who had both obtained seniority and a professional social work qualification, a third had attained a senior position within five years of qualifying, a third had taken from five to nine years and a fifth had taken 10 years or more. Qualified women had taken longer to reach their first senior post than men. Thus, among qualified senior social work staff (team leaders, team managers and senior social workers), 68% of women but 83% of men had reached their first senior post within five years of qualifying ($p<0.01$); put another way, the mean time from qualifying to the first senior post was 8.7 years for women but 6.6 years for men ($p<0.01$). It seems clear, therefore, that age, educational level and possession of a professional social work qualification assist the attainment of seniority, but in gender-specific ways. Professionally qualified women take longer to achieve seniority than similarly qualified men, and overall fewer women possess the educational qualifications associated with seniority.

The review of previous research suggested that part-time working is an important factor in explaining women's relative lack of seniority. In the English study, for example, women were much less likely to work full-time than men (51% compared with 91%, $p<0.001$). In the British workforce as a whole, 93% of employed men work full-time, compared with 56% of women (ONS, 1997).

Table 7.4 shows that staff employed full-time were much more likely than part-timers to hold a senior post. It is only in field social work that a significant proportion of part-timers were senior, and this did not apply in the Scottish study.

Table 7.4: Percentages of staff who were senior in each occupational category, by whether employed full or part-time

	Field social work	Home care	Residential	Central
Full-time				
England	28	13	11	4
Scotland	22	9	5	3
Northern Ireland	27	–	14	9
Part-time				
England	12	1	1	0
Scotland	2	1	0	0
Northern Ireland	17	–	0	0

The findings on career breaks since entry to social care were more complex. Chapter Two has already shown the predominance of career breaks among women and therefore Table 7.5 reports the data on career breaks among senior staff for women only.

Table 7.5: Percentages of women who were senior in each occupational category, by whether they had taken a career break since first employed in social care

	Field social work	Home care	Residential	Central
Career break				
England	28	4	8	3
Scotland	18	4	3	0
Northern Ireland	17	–	10	0
No career break				
England	19	4	7	1
Scotland	9	3	4	1
Northern Ireland	22	–	11	4

In contrast to the findings from previous research, there appears to be no association between career break and limited occupational attainment among women social services staff. With the exception of women field social work staff in Northern Ireland, the attainment of seniority was more common among women who had taken such a break than among those who had not. More detailed analysis of the group most likely to achieve seniority, field social work staff, showed that those who had taken a career break were much younger when they entered social care than those who had not taken a break. The mean age at entry to social care for those who had taken a career break was 23 in England and 24.5 in Scotland, compared with 33 and 35 for those who had not. In England and Scotland, therefore, it appears that women field social work staff who entered social care at a younger age may have acquired the years of experience necessary to attain seniority, and possibly the means to pay for childcare, permitting a rapid return to paid work. This suggests that, by starting their professional occupation before having children, some relatively highly qualified women may be able to circumvent the career disadvantage that applies to women who enter a professional occupation after bearing children, a development recently identified in other work (Glover and Arber, 1995; Macran et al, 1996). In Northern Ireland, the mean ages at entry were much closer at 22 and 26, and those with a career break were slightly disadvantaged in attaining seniority compared with those who had not.

The literature suggests career aspirations vary by gender, and in the English Workforce studies we explored differences in the readiness of women and men to stay in work whether or not the income was necessary to lead a comfortable life. There were no differences between women and men in this respect, with just over half prepared to continue working (Ginn et al, 1997). Nor were there differences between full- and part-time staff, except in field social work, where perhaps surprisingly, 41% of full-time staff but only 20% of part-time workers would give up work. When asked about their aspirations to move into management, there were gender differences in home care and residential work. Although 70% of male staff in home care and residential work saw themselves moving into management, this was true of only 25% of women home care staff and 41% of women residential staff (McLean, 1995). Among social work staff, however, there were no differences between men and women, echoing Taylor's original finding among social work students (Taylor, 1994). Thus differences in career aspirations may form part of the explanation for the under-representation of women in senior posts in home care and residential work, but not in field social work.

The analysis so far has explored each factor in isolation, while in reality women's careers are influenced by a number of factors in concert. Regression analysis was used to identify the most influential combination of factors affecting seniority and Table 7.6 shows them for each job type in each of the studies (for further details, see Ginn and Buglass, 1996; Ginn, et al, 1996; Ginn et al, 1997).

Table 7.6: Factors influencing seniority

Occupational category	England	Scotland	Northern Ireland
Field social work	Full-time years in social care Educational level	Full-time years in social care –	Full-time years in social care Professional qualification
Home care	Full-time years in social care Number of jobs in social services Educational level	Full-time years in social care Number of jobs in social services –	– –
Residential	Full-time years in social care Professional qualification	Full-time years in social care Professional qualification	– Professional qualification
Central	Educational level –	Full-time years in social care –	Full-time years in social care Professional qualification

The key issue to note from this table is the absence of gender – in other words, gender did not combine with other factors to influence the attainment of seniority to any significant degree. This shows that once account has been taken of differences attributable to factors such as full-time years of social care employment educational or professional qualifications, being a woman or a man did not affect the likelihood of holding a senior position.

Length of full–time service is clearly a critical factor, and indeed outweighs the influence of professional qualifications even in field social work where such qualifications might be thought to be the dominant factor. Only in the attainment of seniority among residential staff in

Northern Ireland did professional qualifications play a more important role, perhaps reflecting the drive in Northern Ireland to improve the level of professional qualifications among this staff group. Full-time service also outweighed the effect of educational qualifications, except for central and strategic staff in the English study.

The implication of these findings is that discrimination against women is more likely to be indirect than direct. In other words, it is less likely to be the fact of being a woman that prevents the attainment of seniority, than women's shorter average full-time experience, combined with their lower educational and professional qualifications. This represents indirect discrimination, because women as a group are more likely to experience the domestic constraints which result in part-time and fragmented employment patterns.

Conclusions

At the outset, this chapter suggested that social services agencies have two reasons to review their policies and practices for the promotion of women to senior positions – the need to maximise the potential of their workforce, and to fulfil their role in challenging discrimination. The data show that women do continue to experience disadvantage in attaining seniority, but that this results from factors other than direct discrimination. These include lower qualifications, but the picture is dominated by the influence of full-time service. Unless this factor can be changed, women's career progression will continue to be impeded, no matter how assiduous the accumulation of qualifications. Although others have argued that women and men differ in their career orientations, our research found little difference between women and men in their commitment to the job. In addition, the aspiration for seniority was equally evident among women field social work staff, the main job type possessing the educational and professional qualifications equipping them to compete with men for managerial advancement.

There is a clear relationship between the two factors that need to be addressed in order to remove the barriers limiting career progression for women – the role of family responsibilities and the role of full-time service in career history. A career history with substantial full-time service is clearly less easy for women to achieve while they retain principal responsibility for childcare. Although it is encouraging that some professionally qualified women are able to overcome the traditional disadvantage of a career break, we also have evidence from the Workforce studies that the stress levels are higher for women with young children who work full-time than for their male colleagues (Ginn and Sandell, 1997). This suggests that women whose career pattern closely resembles that of men may be paying a higher cost in terms of stress, since they also carry greater responsibilities at home.

The key may be to change the way we conceive of 'career', and to redefine it so that the skills and experience women gain in unpaid work are valued and specifically included in the abilities sought in senior positions. There are good reasons for doing so in addition to maximising the workforce potential and challenging discrimination. The experience of caring for children or other adults, which is widespread among the social services workforce (Balloch et al, 1997), might be seen as an asset rather than as an obstacle to effective performance. It provides first-hand experience of the issues many service users face, which, if properly integrated into education and training, provides social services workers with additional understanding and credibility. Knight also argues from her qualitative research that key managerial skills, such as problem-solving, risk-taking, and planning are enhanced by the experience of motherhood (Knight, 1994).

The argument here is that there should be a parallel between the public role of social services to promote the interests of women and those they look after (who form the majority of service users), and the organisational concern to ensure that the skills and abilities of women are valued. The more effectively the organisation is able to employ and maximise the abilities of women in the workforce, the greater the likelihood that the workforce will provide relevant and effective services to women and those they look after. This change in organisational culture would thus enhance the quality of front-line services.

A comprehensive human resources strategy, in which women's life experiences are reflected in recruitment, access to education and training, career planning, confidence building, assertiveness training, and stress management (McDougall, 1996), would advance women's careers and strengthen the contribution they make to social services. As Coyle suggests, it would recognise the need "not to be equal with men in any simple sense but to build employment practices which are equally informed by women's experiences" (Coyle and Skinner, 1988).

EIGHT

Education and training in social work and social care

Susan Balloch

Introduction

While training is primarily oriented to equipping staff to do the job as currently defined, education has the broader role of enabling staff to think critically and respond to new demands and new circumstances with confidence. It is education and training together which can create a flexible workforce. Current concern over training standards is a direct result of scandals and tragedies judged to result from the lack of training and poor practice of front-line staff and their managers. In both England and Northern Ireland major reports have implicated the lack of training of residential staff in the abuse of children in residential care (Hughes, 1986 et al; Utting, 1991). In social work heavily publicised cases of child abuse and neglect have criticised training as well as emphasising other failures, such as inter-agency collaboration, to which effective training could have made a difference. More recently research has illustrated the mismatch between the practice and competency of newly qualified social workers and the expectations of their employers (Marsh and Triseliotis, 1996). Training should not, however, be viewed in isolation from the other factors which affect management and practice in the social services, such as adequate staffing, funding, policies, procedures and a supportive working environment (Horwath, 1996).

In the early 1990s, in response to the perceived need to improve and replenish the skills of the workforce, major changes were made in both qualifying training and in training not leading to a qualification. In qualifying training the Diploma in Social Work (DipSW) replaced both the Certificate of Qualification in Social Work (CQSW) and the Certificate in Social Services (CSS). Other initiatives included Post-Qualifying training (PQ), the Residential Child Care Initiative (RCCI) and National or Scottish Vocational Qualifications (NVQs and SVQs). There was also an increasing emphasis on management courses available from universities and other bodies. Training not leading to a qualification saw a growth of short courses provided on a wide range of issues by both in-house and external training bodies. More recently a government policy review in 1997 and the subsequent White Paper (Secretary of State 1998, Cm 4169) have decided that the development, regulation and awarding functions of the Central Council for Education and Training in Social Work (CCETSW) should be carried out in the future by a General Social Care Council (GSCC). CCETSW will be partially replaced by a National Training Organisation (NTO) for the personal social services, to be called TOPSS – Training Organisation for Personal Social Services. Separate regulatory bodies will be set up for England, Scotland, Northern Ireland and Wales. Among the eighty or so other NTOs that will come on stream within the next year, several could also have important implications for the training of social work and social care staff. These include NTOs for health care, early years, community development, advice and guidance, housing, the voluntary sector and community justice.

The last decade has also seen a determined effort to introduce a more strategic approach to the management and resourcing of training. In England, apart from separate CCETSW bursaries for DipSW courses, funding for training is provided by the Training Support Programme (TSP) Grant first made available to social services departments in 1988 in acknowledgement of the concern over the numbers of untrained staff in residential homes for older people. This was eventually widened to include other staff working with older people, childcare staff and management. In 1995/96 the TSP grant amounted to £34.55m. As it is available to social services departments on a 70:30 basis (that is, with departments providing 30%) estimated expenditure on training was £48.9m (SSI, 1997).

In Scotland a Specific Grant for Training was introduced by the Scottish Office in 1992. In 1995/96 this amounted to £4.3m, of which £27,000 was ring-fenced for practice placements. As in England, social work departments contribute a matching 30% to Specific Grant Funding. The purpose of the grant is for training delivery costs, fees, staff replacement costs and material and design costs. It is targeted towards community care and services to children and families and, as in England, intended to be additional to training already provided from social work departments' mainstream budgets. Scottish social work departments also provide services to the criminal justice system and social work training within criminal justice is financed from the Scottish Office Criminal Justice Grant. As in England, CCETSW funds students following DipSW courses.

In Northern Ireland the DHSS allocates training funds to statutory employers in accordance with the Chief Social Services Inspector's Circular 'Personal social services training strategy: securing the objectives' (July 1995). Such training funds include support for NVQ training, DipSW training and PQ.

In the social services, where training strategies are usually led by employers, two crucial issues are often neglected. The first concerns those who use social services. We know from other studies that the right training for staff can make a substantial difference to service users. For example, a long-term study of small houses for people with learning difficulties showed that good standards of provision and progress for clients could not be maintained without continued development of staff skill and commitment (Mansell and Beasley, 1993). Yet current training programmes may isolate users: Dominelli (1996) has argued that an emphasis on competencies in training fragments social work and social care tasks and impedes a holistic view of individuals' or groups' needs; it also acts as a distraction from the severe disadvantages and discrimination experienced by different types of users and prevents these being recognised within standards setting and training. Service users are also largely excluded from the training process itself. Although it has been established that users have clear ideas of what they want from services and have little difficulty in engaging with the current debate on 'outcomes' (Harding and Beresford, 1996; Turner, 1997), their involvement in the setting of standards and in the development of training is still at an early stage. In an overview of social services departments' training plans it was noted that:"Few plans identified outcomes for training and even fewer described how these training outcomes were intended to contribute to better outcomes for service users and carers" (SSI, 1997, p 42).

The second issue draws attention to the importance of a lifelong approach to learning. The development of a skilled and competent workforce is an important goal, but pursuit of this to the satisfaction of employers may ignore the longer-term educational needs of workers. Employers are answerable to a wide range of legislation and directives and have been publicly pilloried for failure either to train staff, or employ trained staff, appropriately. They want to be seen to be protecting service users and the public through their training programmes. Employees, however, need more than accredited training, both for their own development and to meet the needs of users and carers effectively. As shown later, to do their job they rely heavily on skills which have not been acquired through conventional training, as well as on their own experience of life. To meet the changing needs of service users and employers, and to advance their own careers, they require further opportunities which we can broadly describe as educational. Overall, staff need to develop a lifelong approach to learning and be supported in this by their employers. However, while our findings suggest that most of those working in the social services do want a continuum of education and training, they also show that this is only available to a minority. For the majority of residential and home care workers neither education nor relevant training is readily available.

We cannot pretend that the diverse demands and needs of employers, social services users and social services staff can be easily reconciled. If, however, an attempt is not made through education and training programmes to address these, the future quality of social care will offer little improvement on the present.

Evidence on education and training from the Workforce studies

In the first interview, we looked at the training experiences of the four main job types – managers, field social work staff, home care workers and residential workers (Balloch et al, 1995). We identified very positive attitudes among staff towards both qualifying and non-qualifying training, but found that, in spite of the TSP Grant, access to training was very uneven. Whereas a majority of field social work staff and managers held a professional qualification, this was only true of very few residential workers and almost no home care workers. Information on courses was also far more readily available to managers and field social work staff, though obtaining time off to study and back up from colleagues while studying was difficult. The data on non-qualifying training was impressive, showing that social services staff appeared to receive more in service training than those in other occupations (Buck et al, 1994).

In the second interview, in addition to qualifying and non-qualifying training courses, staff were asked about other methods through which they thought they had learnt the skills needed for their current job. Our main findings, and the experiences of training of those who remained with the same employer between interviews, form the substance of this chapter.

Learning to do the job

It has been argued that because "All forms of questions which use *train* or *training* would appear to restrict respondents' replies and lead to under-reporting" it is preferable to phrase questions about skill acquisition very broadly (Campanelli and Channell, 1994). These give the researcher the chance to find out more about how individuals think they learn the skills needed for their work. In the second interview we therefore asked a question similar to one used in the Department of Employment's 'Family and Working Lives Survey': 'Thinking about the skills you need to do your current job, did you acquire these skills through any of the following methods and how helpful were these?'

In all three samples managers and field social work staff defined the same four methods as most helpful. These were:

- general experience of life, such as how to deal with people and get things done;
- actually doing the job, job experience;
- getting help from more experienced people;
- going on a course for a work-related qualification.

These were also the most common choices for residential workers, except in Scotland where going on a course for a work related qualification was seen as less helpful. For home care staff the personal experience gained from running one's own household was rated almost as highly as the first three methods and qualifying courses received few votes. Thus the least support for taking qualifications was found among the least qualified staff.

For all staff the least popular ways of acquiring skills included: learning things at school, studying after leaving school, spending time in different units learning about the organisation, doing things for practice with an instructor correcting mistakes and doing unpaid voluntary work.

Gender differences in this context were not assessed for home care workers as the number of men was very small. Among the other three job types, women tended to find some methods of learning more helpful than men, such as doing things for practice with an instructor correcting mistakes, going to talks and demonstrations, and spending time in other units learning about the organisation. Arguably these are fairly structured learning modes. Women social work staff and residential workers also attached greater value to the skills learnt bringing up children and running their own home. That there was little difference between women and men managers may suggest a difference between 'career women' and other women. As women themselves attach considerable value to the skills gained from their unpaid work, should not employers be more prepared to take these into account when recruiting staff? (see also Chapter Seven).

In England, black and white staff were very similar in their reporting of methods of learning in all aspects except one. Fifty-two per cent of black staff responding to the question on studying books thought that this was a very helpful method of learning, but only 31% of white staff. This finding fits in with the first interviews which showed black staff more likely to be studying for qualifications and to be studying on their own at home.

There were some interesting differences, and similarities, between younger and older workers which could have considerable implications for training programmes. Younger workers were much less likely than older workers to place value on non-qualifying courses or traditionally structured learning practices. Understandably, they also set less store in bringing up children, running their own home and life experiences. In common with other workers, they saw their main methods of skill acquisition in actually doing the job, getting help from more experienced people and studying for work-related qualifications. Older workers, as expected, saw their life experiences, including running a home and bringing up children, as valuable, but assigned equal importance with young people to work related qualifications. Given the difficulties faced by older workers in obtaining qualifying training (Itzin and Phillipson, 1993), this finding warrants further consideration in training programmes.

In the last decade the effectiveness of classroom type teaching for workforce training has been called into question and moves made within the social services and elsewhere towards work-based or experiential learning programmes. Our research confirms that staff value this approach, although home care and residential workers were just as likely to favour special talks and demonstrations. We recognise, however, that tensions still exist between experiential and more formalised, didactic procedures, with a tendency for reversion to the conventional teaching and learning models where the demands for workplace supervision and support cannot easily be met (Darvill, 1996) or where staff are looking for a secure 'ivory tower' environment (Hughes and Pengelly, 1995, p 154). Our findings suggest that such tensions should not be allowed to detract from the learning methods that staff recognise as most valuable. They also call into question the current emphasis placed on employment experience at the expense of other experiences, such as bringing up children or running a home, or life skills acquired through other personal experiences, particularly in the recruitment of older workers.

It is interesting to reflect on the value of the most popular methods of learning to a workforce faced with extensive changes at work. Reliance on general experience of life, job experience and getting help from more experienced people for skills acquisition could be assessed as essentially conservative approaches, more concerned with passing on tried and tested techniques and 'common sense' than with developing new skills, and, more importantly, the knowledge required, to understand and act appropriately in changing situations. Given the current debate on 'evidence-based', or as we would prefer to call it, 'knowledge-based' practice (Fisher, 1997), the value of good training is unquestionable. By 'good' training we mean that which is broadly based on relevant and up-to-date research and takes into account the knowledge and expertise of service users, as well as the accumulated experience of managers and front-line staff in both social services and other related agencies such as housing and health. Although user-led training programmes are not widely used, they can prove very effective in putting users' interests at the heart of training (Lindow and Morris, 1995). Such training has a unique potential to be dynamic, enabling individuals to challenge their taken for granted experiences and prepare themselves thoughtfully for new roles.

Interest in training

In all three study areas most staff demonstrated substantial and similar levels of interest in training. This interest was sustained between interviews, as were the differences between job types (Table 8.1). Managers and field social work staff, the most qualified of the workforce, were the most interested in non-qualifying training and residential staff the most interested in gaining qualifications. While a substantial minority of home care staff in England and Scotland said they were not interested in training of any sort, this turned out to be the majority in Northern Ireland. This finding may have been partly related to the older ages of home care staff, while residential staff's interest in qualifying training may have been related to their relative youth (See Chapter Two).

Table 8.1: Level of interest in training: percentages by job type

Job type	Not very interested	Interested in training not for qualifications	Interested in training for qualification
Manager			
England	1	51	48
Scotland	0	58	42
Northern Ireland	4	64	32
Field social work staff			
England	2	58	40
Scotland	0	47	53
Northern Ireland	4	52	44
Home care staff			
England	20	46	34
Scotland	28	30	42
Northern Ireland	66	17	17
Residential worker			
England	13	46	53
Scotland	21	24	55
Northern Ireland	4	31	65

In Northern Ireland the home help sample was not representative of the whole population of home helps, as two Trusts in the Eastern Health and Social Services Board did not provide listings of home helps. The sampling fraction was also much smaller than in England and Scotland because of the larger number of home care workers in Northern Ireland (Chapter One). In this home care sample only 7% of the home care staff worked 30 hours per week or more and 28% worked 10 hours per week or less. The low level of interest in training varied little, however, according to the hours worked.

Differences between black and white staff in England were marked, with 65% of black staff compared with 39% of white staff more likely to be interested in training for qualifications. This difference was significant and was true for black staff in all job types after taking into consideration gender, age and employing authority. Holding a social work qualification did not affect their interest in further qualifications. One explanation for this would be the advantage that black staff see in qualifications in career advancement. The greater value that black staff, in comparison with white staff, appear to place on gaining qualifications, may result from their perception that this is one way of assisting career attainment in the face of racism and discrimination (see also Chapter Six).

A further explanation for the widespread interest in both qualifying and non-qualifying training may lie in the genuine commitment of staff to their work and the satisfaction gained from it (see Chapter Four), something to which we will return later in this chapter. In the meantime we will look at some of the evidence from the Workforce studies on the take-up of different types of training, key issues affecting training and the extent to which demand for training is being met.

Professional qualifications

The proportions of staff who held a recognised social work qualification at second interview are given in Table 8.2. The findings for England and Scotland are very similar, but in sharp contrast to those for Northern Ireland where the percentage of qualified staff is substantially higher. One possible reason for this difference is that people with job titles such as social work assistant, project worker and community care assistant, who would not normally be qualified, were included within the broad departmental classification of field social work staff together with qualified workers. However, in Northern Ireland at second interview, 30% of social work assistants were qualified compared with 12% in England. Among managers, the much higher percentage in Northern Ireland with a social work qualification may indicate a career progression from social work into management less strongly developed in England and Scotland.

Table 8.2: Percentages of each job type professionally qualified in social work at second interview

	Managers	Field social work staff	Residential workers
Second interview			
England	51	77	4
Scotland	56	70	7
Northern Ireland	85	89	25

We are led to the conclusion that Northern Ireland's social services are staffed by a higher proportion of qualified staff than in England and Scotland. This could be the result of a determined policy of training which set targets for qualification and the stability of the workforce over this period (51% of the Northern Ireland sample of qualified workers obtained their qualifications before 1985 compared with 38% of the

English sample). It may also reflect a generally higher level of educational attainment in the Northern Ireland population. At first interview, 50% of managers, 63% of field social work staff and 13% of residential workers held first or higher degrees in Northern Ireland, compared with 35% of managers, 35% of field social work staff and 6% of residential workers in England, and 31% of managers, 47% of field social work staff, and 5% of residential workers in Scotland (see also McConkey, 1998; McLean and Andrew, 1998).

Looking more closely at field social work staff, in England and Scotland at second interview over 90% of those whose main user group was children and families were qualified, indicating that the recent emphasis on qualifying training for those working in child protection had been successful. In both countries, however, a lower percentage of qualified field social work staff was found among those responsible for older people, with about 75% in England and 46% in Scotland qualified. This questions how far qualification is pursued with equal determination in relation to work with different groups of social services users.

Among field social work staff, women, black staff and those over the age of 40 were more likely to be unqualified. In Northern Ireland there were striking gender differences in levels of qualification: among managers and field social work staff, all men were qualified but 21% and 15% respectively of women were unqualified (McConkey, 1998). In England job titles suggested that unqualified field social work staff were acting in supportive roles as, for example, social work assistants, community care officers, access workers and project workers. Their presence in the field social work sample is indicative of the wide parameters of social work resulting from the diverse demands made by the changing needs of different social groups. It may also indicate that non-qualified staff in the social services are particularly valued for their maturity and experience, in spite of their lack of a formal qualification (Dobson, 1996). (See Chapter Seven for a more detailed discussion of the relationship between gender, qualifications and career advancement.)

Educational and professional qualifications

In England about 5% of staff obtained an educational qualification between interviews. In Scotland and Northern Ireland the percentage was lower at 3% though actual achievement was probably the same or similar given the shorter period between interviews. Managers and field social work staff were the most likely to have obtained first or higher degrees.

The main work related qualifications for which people had been studying in the 12 months before interview were social work qualifications (Degree in Social Work, DipSW and CQSW), post-qualifying certificates (PQs), NVQs/SVQs and management qualifications.

Social work qualifications

Among managers, field social work staff and residential staff, numbers taking or obtaining social work qualifications were very small. In England only seven individuals said they had obtained a qualification between interviews. In Northern Ireland 18 individuals had taken or were studying for a social work qualification. The low numbers prevented a comparison with the findings of Marsh and Triseliotis (1996) survey of the readiness to practise of social workers who had completed the DipSW course.

By the second interview the percentage of qualified social workers who had taken or were currently taking a post-qualifying course had risen to 33% in England, 47% in Scotland and 54% in Northern Ireland. The range of qualifications was varied and some had gained or were working towards more than one qualification.

Mental health qualifications

Changes in the care of those with mental health problems has raised concern over the supply of adequate numbers of qualified, approved social workers (ASWs) in England and Northern Ireland and mental health officers (MHOs) in Scotland. In 1995, 44% of English authorities replying to the annual Local Government Management Board (LGMB) survey reported that their numbers were inadequate to meet responsibilities under the 1983 Mental Health Act, blaming recruitment and retention difficulties and pressure of work (LGMB, 1996). The survey found that 17% of all field social workers were ASWs, but that this was 5% lower than in 1994.

At the second interview we focused on these qualifications, asking those with a social work qualification if they were also qualified as an ASW. Similarly to the LGMB survey, 18% said yes, of whom a quarter had obtained their qualification since their first interview. However, at second interview, of those who were qualified as ASWs, less than half were working in a post for which an ASW qualification was required. In Northern Ireland 20% said they were approved social work staff, but of these 70% said they were working in posts where this was necessary. In Scotland 27% of qualified social workers were MHOs and about two thirds of these were working in a job which required MHO qualifications.

Management training

About a quarter of managers in England, Scotland and Northern Ireland had taken or were studying for a management qualification. Reactions to management courses were very favourable with high percentages describing these as helpful in enabling them to do their job better, improving their confidence and career prospects, building up a network of contacts, gaining new skills and, in particular, helping to improve the quality of service provided.

National Vocational Qualifications

Social work training has become increasingly regulated with the passage of time, mainly to meet the changing priorities established by central government (Payne, 1995; Humphries, 1997). The content of training has been a product of those responsible – professionals, academics and other agencies – and their changing commitment to different theories and approaches. The current emphasis on 'competencies' and the search for standards can be seen as the latest in a long line of attempts to exert greater control over the methods and quality of social work and social care practice. Recently this has been extended to the large group of social care workers who are unqualified. The vehicle for this has been the system of accreditation for NVQs and SVQs.

NVQS and SVQs were introduced in Care, Child Care and Education to raise the competence and certification of unqualified staff, such as home care and residential workers. In all three samples at first interview their take up in the statutory social services was low, with social services departments in England, for example, accounting for only 3% of NVQ awards granted in these areas in 1994/95 (Care Sector Consortium, 1996).

Home care and residential workers were asked if they thought they could be assessed for NVQs/SVQs through their employer. By their second interview, most staff had become more aware of the possibilities of assessment although the general level of awareness among home care workers in Northern Ireland remained very low. Increased awareness was presumably a result of staff being better informed, or indeed because of the effects of the survey.

Increased awareness had not resulted in much improved uptake. At second interview, only about 10% of residential and home care workers in England were taking or held an NVQ and in Northern Ireland, though 20% of unqualified residential workers were taking an NVQ, the percentage of home care staff had fallen from 2% at first interview to nil. Only in Scotland did there appear to have been some real growth, with 24% of residential staff and 11% of home care staff taking an SVQ by their second interview.

Most NVQs/SVQs were held or were being taken at level 2. A majority said they had been encouraged to take the qualification and had found the assessment process fair. They thought their qualification was very helpful in enabling them to do their job better, improve the quality of service, raise self-confidence, increase career prospects and gain new skills.

A member of the English panel, who had left his post as a care bank residential worker for permanent employment as a residential worker in another authority, commented on NVQ assessments in a telephone interview. He had been doing levels one and two of Direct Care, which involved about two days NVQ work a month plus a half an hour meeting fortnightly. He thought it was a 'brilliant scheme' and hoped to continue to level 3 in the future. As the assessments were just being introduced, however, he found the goal posts kept changing. Having set out to do things one way, he then found that the suggested best way to reach a target had changed, or the time-scale had changed, illustrating the confusion that marks many new training procedures and causes uncertainty in the early months of new courses.

Overall, however, interest in NVQs\SVQs remained disappointing. Achievement of awards continues to be a slow process, competing with other training opportunities and the combined pressures of work and family life.

Training not leading to a qualification

Enthusiasm for short course training (training lasting less than a week and not related to a qualification) is widespread in the social services. At both interviews, a large majority of the managers, field social work staff and residential staff in England, Scotland and Northern Ireland had undertaken such training in the 12 months prior to the interview. This was not true of home care staff, of whom only about a third in England

and Scotland and only 6% in Northern Ireland had taken any such courses (Table 8.3). However, in Scotland the percentage of home care workers taking short courses had doubled between interviews.

Table 8.3: Participation in training not leading to a qualification in the 12 months before the second interview: percentages by job type

	Managers	Field social work staff	Home care workers	Residential workers
England	86	86	42	70
Scotland	90	75	31	67
Northern Ireland	88	83	6	79

Many had taken more than one course, usually within working hours. Popular courses included those in general management, recruitment, computing, child protection, mental health and dealing with aggression. Eighteen per cent in England and Northern Ireland and 17% in Scotland had taken courses relating to work in adult community care. Examples of courses attended by home care staff in England and Scotland were mental health, community work and lifting and handling, suggesting that some staff were becoming involved in work with more dependent users who required personal care or who had specific needs beyond traditional home care support such as shopping and cleaning. In England only 1% named courses related to issues of current concern such as equal opportunities, stress management, welfare rights and advocacy.

Most saw short courses as very helpful or helpful in enabling them to do their job better, improve the quality of service provided, improve confidence and gain new skills. About half thought they helped build up a network of contacts and improved understanding of equal opportunities but only a third saw them as improving career prospects. Most courses were provided by the employing authority and few through joint training with outside agencies.

Individual commitment to study was also confirmed with responses to a question about work related courses based on self-study using workbooks, audio tape or video. About 10% of staff in all three countries at both interviews said they were taking such courses in their own time. In England black staff were more likely than white staff to have been involved with self-study, (13% compared with 7% of white staff). Older staff were also more likely candidates than younger staff, with 68% being over the age of forty.

Difficulties in obtaining training

In spite of the amount of training that had been taking place, over two fifths of staff in each sample said that in the 12 months prior to their second interview, there had been training which they would have liked to have done but had been unable to do. As in the first interview, difficulty accessing training was more likely to have been mentioned by those most commonly receiving training, that is those under 40 years, social workers and managers, suggesting that training itself stimulates further demand for courses. Courses most frequently in demand were in management, counselling, childcare, mental illness, the DipSW and NVQ/SVQ courses for home care and residential staff in England and Scotland.

The reasons most commonly given for not being able to attend a course were being too busy, concern about off-loading work onto others, and not being allowed time off or funding for fees. These reasons were similar to findings from first and second interviews about the amount of help staff received with their workload when studying for work-related qualifications. Although this had improved between interviews, most managers and field social work staff did not receive much support while training and were expected to catch up with their work later. This was confirmed in England by a Social Services Inspectorate report which found that social services departments were reluctant to release staff for training because they could not afford cover (DoH, 1996b).

Some staff may have been waiting some time for training. In their first interview staff were asked if there was training they would have liked but had been unable to do. Of those who said yes, only a third in England and Scotland and 43% in Northern Ireland had taken this training between interviews. This reinforces our evidence that there is substantial demand for training in the social services which at the time of our survey was not being met.

Training experiences of those who changed jobs/job titles

To see how well prepared they were when starting their new job, questions were addressed specifically to those in the sample who, while not moving out of their employing authority, had changed job or job title between interviews – 28% of the English sample, 24% of the Scottish sample and 18% of the Northern Ireland sample of managers, field social work staff and residential workers.

Table 8.4: Training experiences of those who changed job/ job title between interviews: percentages of whole samples

	Very well prepared for new job	Received extra supervision and support	Received initial training
England	79	35	32
Scotland	85	39	27
Northern Ireland	80	48	26

Table 8.4 shows that a large majority said they felt very well prepared for their new job, even though less than half received extra supervision and support and less than a third received initial training. The more senior the staff, the less support and training they seem to have received. In England, for example, among the managers, team leaders and home care organisers, a majority lacked support and training. In Scotland 25% of managers received supervision/support and 21% introductory training compared with 61% and 40% respectively of field social workers. In Northern Ireland 23% of social work managers and officers in charge reported receiving supervision/support compared with 43% of social work staff and 56% of residential workers.

In a study of the impact of community care reforms on front-line staff and their managers, 59% of team managers reported wanting more management training on issues such as policy and strategy, managing change positively, staff supervision and support, team building, motivating staff, coping with low staff morale, managing staff absences, recruitment, selection and complaints procedures. Demand was attributed to the changes in the roles and tasks of team managers with the introduction of devolved budgets and purchasing. The team managers had indicated that the progression from experienced social worker to team manager was a difficult one to make and a proper induction to the job and learning opportunities were limited. A team manager was quoted as saying "General management training – it's all done on the job at present – no departmental training for new managers" (Levin and Webb, 1997).

Training, job mobility and commitment to work

We were interested in possible relationships between the ambitions of staff (to stay in the same or a similar job, change jobs or be promoted, or do something else), and qualifying and non-qualifying training and, in an initial analysis for Scotland, uncovered compelling evidence of a strong relationship between ambition and training (Buglass et al, 1998). Those who sought a job change were more likely to take up training opportunities than those who were content to stay in the same job, and those who had undertaken training, particularly qualifying training, appeared more likely to look for a new job or actually to make a move. For example, of those who had taken courses leading to a qualification prior to the first interview, 42% had applied for a new job compared with 16% who had not taken such a course; of those who had taken non-qualifying training, 25% had applied for a new job compared with 16% who had not taken such training. Residential workers who had undertaken qualifying training were twice as likely as those not receiving training to have applied for a new job.

The nature of the relationship between training, aspirations and job change is by no means clear. Participation in qualifying training may logically imply a future job change (in that the staff member may become eligible after training for a wider range of jobs) and training itself may assist in creating the ability to change jobs and, in turn, feed aspirations. For others changing jobs may be only marginally related to the training undertaken if the driving force is one of organisational change (see Chapter Nine). Training probably makes for a more mobile workforce and, in the short term, may work against an individual employer's human resources strategy if staff turnover rises. However, the turnover of social services staff, at around 9% each year, is not particularly high and, as shown in Chapter Two, managers and field social work staff change jobs relatively frequently by moving within social services rather than by leaving. Training can therefore be seen as a resource for the whole workforce, facilitating the accumulation of experience as well as competence.

There is also some evidence that training enhances commitment to work. For newcomers initial training can provide both a socialising and reassuring process, with newly found feelings of competence playing a role in the development of affective commitment. Research has also established a link between organisational commitment and the motivation to take up training (Meyer and Allen, 1997). The substantial interest in training expressed by a large majority of the social services workforce may well be linked to the commitment to social work and social care expressed in responses to our survey.

Conclusions

In the social services professional qualifications are valued for conferring skills and career opportunities, but are not seen as a substitute for the maturity and life skills which facilitate communication with social services users and an understanding of their needs. The attitudes of social services staff to training reflect this thinking. In addition to qualifying training courses and training courses not leading to a qualification, older workers in particular place considerable value on their life experiences, actually doing the job and working with more experienced staff. These are valuable and important avenues of learning which need to be given proper recognition, particularly by those in charge of staff recruitment. However, these methods of learning rely heavily on past experience and current practice and cannot prepare either managers or the rest of the workforce for new working systems and new practices. This is where education and training becomes essential, both for strategy development and learning new procedures and techniques. It is why training is so important during the present period of rapid change.

Our evidence revealed striking similarities in the keen interest of staff in training, with the exception of some home care workers, particularly in Northern Ireland. While managers and field social workers placed equal value on qualifying and non-qualifying training, there was a considerable imbalance between access to these which became more pronounced by the second interview. In England, for example, 15% of staff were taking qualifying courses, in comparison with 64% taking other courses; in Scotland the respective percentages were 30% and 53%; in Northern Ireland 26% and 84% (excluding home care staff). This surely created problems for staff such as residential workers, and black staff in England, whose main interest was in gaining qualifications. Our findings also showed a majority of managers without a management qualification, and about a quarter of field social work staff in England and Scotland and the majority of home care workers and residential workers unqualified. Education and training strategies need to reassess this situation.

A workforce in a period of rapid change is likely to see increased staff mobility. Our evidence suggests that about a third of those changing jobs were unlikely to receive the support and supervision necessary to prepare them properly for new roles. This was particularly true of more senior staff. These were, on the whole, older workers, and we need to challenge the assumption that older workers will be able to cope with new situations because of their life experiences. As argued earlier, it is only training that can prepare them properly for new situations.

In analysing the first interviews we noted the unequal access to information on training, and to training opportunities, of different job types. Such inequalities had changed little between interviews because the main initiative directed at residential and home care staff, NVQs/SVQs, had not had sufficient impact. There was, however, evidence of progress, particularly among residential staff in Scotland, and hopefully this will gather speed over the next couple of years. It does require a willingness on the part of the employing authorities, however, to allocate sufficient funding and staff time to make NVQs/SVQs viable, as well as interest from staff. This is also true for the development of new forms of training, such as joint training programmes and short courses relevant to community care. Again, there were signs of progress being made, but relatively slowly.

The social services workforce provides value for money, in that its turnover is modest and its staff are committed to their work. Education and training in the social services does not, therefore, involve an investment that will be rapidly dissipated. Rather there is every chance that its accumulated benefits will be put to use in raising standards of service for users and developing the human resources on which the social services depend.

NINE

Moving jobs and staying put

John McLean and Linda Dolan

Most of this book has concentrated on the majority of staff in the three samples who stayed in the same job with the same employer throughout the period covered by the study. This chapter now looks at the minority of staff who changed jobs between interviews.

Movement of staff between jobs can be healthy for organisations, infusing them with fresh blood and enthusiasm and introducing new ways of approaching old problems (Knapp et al, 1981). However, if a balance is not struck between staff's aspirations to change jobs and continuity of care, staff leaving may result in a net loss of skills and investment in training, unless the individuals concerned were unable to carry out the work for some reason (Younghusband, 1978). Staff leaving may also involve employers in expensive and time-consuming recruitment, training and induction, and may affect long-term planning and the morale of those who remain.

There are various ways to describe movement between jobs, and any estimate of rates of staff turnover will depend on how job change is defined (Buck et al, 1994). Turnover is generally referred to as staff leaving the employer but staying in the same occupation, while wastage refers to staff who leave the occupation altogether. Although the definitions vary, employers may not necessarily view the two differently since the consequences of staff leaving will be the same, regardless of whether staff stay in the same occupation or not. In the Workforce studies staff who changed jobs after the first interview made one of three types of move: within the same department; to another employer but staying in the field of social care or social services; and to a job or activity outwith social care work.

Because of the implications for service provision, it is important to understand the dynamics of staff movement between jobs and the reasons for doing so. Previous reports from the Workforce studies (Ginn et al, 1997; also Chapters Two and Seven) described a very stable pattern of employment by staff who had a high level of commitment to working for social services. Once employed by social services, most changes involved movement to other social services jobs, usually of the same type, and mostly for the same employer. Staff who left social services were likely to remain in social care work. Home care workers were the least likely to move, whereas managers and field social work staff changed jobs most often, a pattern that was observed in other studies of the social services workforce (LGMB, 1995). Most staff had made an 'active decision' to change jobs, and usually did so because of the attraction of another job, but towards the most recent period, reorganisation had become the main reason for moving (Ginn et al, 1997).

This chapter will examine moves by staff in the period between the interviews. Because of the larger sample size and the longer interval between interviews in England (about two years, compared with 15 to 21 months in Scotland and Northern Ireland), the English sample can be used to provide a broader picture of the extent and nature of job change. Of the 1,276 staff who took part in the first interviews in England, 62% were still in the same job at the second interview. This varied between job types, from 59% of managers and 58% of residential workers to 65% of field social work staff and 67% of home care workers.

Thirty-eight per cent had left the job they were in at the first interview: 20% had moved to another job in the same department and 18% had left the department altogether, either for another job, or for some other reason such as retirement. Since the study covered a two year period, a reasonable estimate of the annual turnover would be 9% (18% over two years), although this figure included wastage, that is staff who left social care altogether. This estimate compares favourably with the level of turnover in other occupations such as nursing (Seccombe and Smith, 1997). The Workforce figures refer to staff who left the job they were in at the first interview, some of whom did not take part in the second interview. As such they are not comparable with Table 2.1 (Chapter Two), which refers to staff who were followed up, some of whom had changed jobs.

There may have been some differences which were due to the longer interval between interviews in England than in Scotland or Northern Ireland, but these were minimal since most questions regarding the circumstances of the move referred to a period such as the previous 12 months. Three groups of staff will be examined: those who had applied for another job in the 12 months before the second interview; those who change jobs within the same department or Board between interviews; and staff who left the department or Board altogether.

Staff who applied for other jobs between the interviews

Those who actually changed jobs between interviews represent part of a larger group of staff who had applied for other jobs, not all of whom were successful. At the first interview, about third said that they were likely to apply for another job in the next year; most likely to say this were men, staff aged less than 40, qualified staff, managers and field social work staff.

A fifth of each sample had applied for another job in the 12 months before the second interview, about twice as many as the proportion who actually moved in this period. Most had applied for only one other job, nearly all in social care. Less than 10% of applications were for other types of work. Most staff had applied for jobs in their own department or Board, between a quarter and a third for jobs with another social services employer, and about 15% had applied for social care jobs in the independent private or voluntary sectors. In other words, most staff who wanted to change jobs did not want to move from their existing employer or from social care work.

As might be expected, more staff who said at the first interview that they intended to apply for other jobs actually did so. Proportions varied considerably between employers, ranging from 12% in an English metropolitan authority to a third in a London borough. These accorded with past job changes by men, managers and social work staff (Ginn et al, 1997) and by different age groups (Buck et al, 1994; Knapp et al, 1981).

Table 9.1 gives details of the types of job applied for between interviews by those who were interviewed twice. This illustrates the extent to which staff wanted to stay in the same type of work, move to management, or do other types of work.

Table 9.1: Type of job applied for: percentages for each sample

Type of job applied for	England	Scotland	Northern Ireland
Same type of job/same or other setting	24	25	31
More senior/not management	20	15	11
Management position	17	24	17
Different job in social care	32	24	36
Job unrelated to social care	8	13	5
sample n	**216**	**74**	**75**

A similar pattern was found in each study area. About a third had applied for the same type of job, a third for a more senior or management job and a third for a different type of job within social care. Men were more likely to have applied for more senior or management positions, whereas women were more likely to have applied for the same type of job. Numbers were too small in Scotland and Northern Ireland to identify any patterns, but in England, more men, particularly in home care and residential work, applied for senior or manager jobs, while more women in field social work, home care and residential work applied for the same type of job. This confirms the pattern described in Chapter Seven of men's ambitions to become managers. About a third of each job type except manager applied for a different kind of social care or social work job. Applications for jobs unrelated to social care were more likely to be made by managers and home care workers.

A fifth of staff in England and Scotland who applied for other jobs and two fifths in Northern Ireland, were offered the job and accepted it. This may partly have been influenced by the fact that a third of job moves in England, and half in Northern Ireland, were due to reorganisation (see Table 9.3 below). Similar proportions of women and men in England and Scotland were offered the job, but in Northern Ireland, women were twice as likely as men to be offered the job. A third of job applicants were interviewed but not appointed; a quarter in England and Scotland but only 8% in Northern Ireland were not short-listed.

In England and Scotland reasons for applying for another job included wanting to do something different, needing a change, wanting promotion, making better use of skills, or lack of motivation or satisfaction in the present job. Although a third had applied for a job in management, very few said they had wanted to develop management skills, and few wanted to work with a different user group. With the exception of home care workers in Scotland, very few staff cited better pay. In contrast, the reasons most often given in Northern Ireland were to develop management skills, to do different work and to work with a different user group.

We need to emphasise that most staff did not apply for other jobs. Satisfaction with the present job was most often the reason for not applying, by 56% of staff in England, 70% in Scotland, and 82% in Northern Ireland. Other reasons for not applying were less positive, for example, feeling that they were too old, or that no suitable jobs were being advertised.

It will be shown later that the attraction of another job was often the reason for moving (see Table 9.3), and many job changes were viewed positively. However, mean GHQ12 scores, which measure stress (see

Chapter Four), were higher at the first interview for staff who applied for other jobs, suggesting that, for some staff, the desire to leave was associated with stress in the existing job. This applied to women and men and to staff in each of the four job types, and may of course indicate that these staff were taking positive action to deal with work they found to be too stressful.

Staff who changed jobs

A fifth of staff in England changed job or job title within the same department in the two years between interviews. In the shorter period between interviews in Scotland, a quarter had changed jobs in the same department while a fifth had done so in the same Board in Northern Ireland. Changes in job titles are included at this stage because they often involved a change in the job description or content. For staff who left the department or Board altogether, where possible a contact address was obtained, and they were invited to take part in a short telephone interview about the circumstances of their departure, and activities afterwards. Examination of these two discrete groups builds on the information provided by the work histories (see Chapter Two) and gives us useful information about the nature of more recent job moves.

Staff who changed jobs but remained with the same employer

Approximately a fifth of staff who were interviewed twice in England and Northern Ireland, and a quarter in Scotland, had changed jobs or job titles within the same department or Board (Table 9.2). Men were more likely to have done this than women, partly reflecting the fact that more job changes involved managers and field social work staff, higher proportions of whom were men. Also more likely to have changed jobs or job title were staff aged less than 40, black staff more than white staff, and staff working for some employers more than others, mainly those which were undergoing internal reorganisation.

Disregarding staff whose job title or job content had changed, most staff who moved to a different job for the same employer between interviews stayed in the same job type, a similar pattern to past job moves (Ginn et al, 1997). Table 9.2 gives the proportions who were still in the same type of job at the second interview.

Table 9.2: Staff who changed jobs in the same authority: percentages who were still in the same job type at the second interview

Job type at first interview	England	Scotland	Northern Ireland
Manager	87	69	78
Field social work staff	56	62	85
Home care worker	78	67	100
Residential worker	69	49	37
sample n	195	58	46

Most staff who left jobs as manager were still in management jobs at the second interview. Those who moved to another job type most frequently became field social work staff, a move made by almost a third of Scottish managers. Most field social work staff who changed jobs stayed in field social work, although this applied to less than two thirds in England and Scotland. Those who changed job type were mostly promoted to manager, particularly in England and Scotland, where this move had been made by a third of field social work staff. Frequencies in Scotland were too low to draw meaningful conclusions, but in England, equal proportions of home care workers who changed job type became home care organisers, other managers or field social work staff. Moves by residential workers in England were to jobs as manager, including officer in charge, and field social work, and although figures were too low in Scotland and Northern Ireland to draw conclusions, residential workers in both samples moved into each of the other three job types.

Most considered that this job move had been the result of an 'active decision' although proportions saying this varied from less than a third in England to 85% in Scotland and 92% in Northern Ireland. Table 9.3 shows the main reasons given by staff who changed jobs within the same department or Board between interviews.

Staff in Scotland were least likely to have changed job through reorganisation and were more likely to have given the attractions of another job as the reason for moving. In contrast, reorganisation was responsible for a third of job changes in England and over half in Northern Ireland, the attractions of another job being the second most frequently given reason in these two samples.

Table 9.3: Main reasons for changing jobs within the same department or Board

Main reason for changing jobs	England	Scotland	Northern Ireland
Reorganisation	37	10	52
Redundancy/(early)retirement	1	0	1
Dissatisfaction	9	17	9
Attraction of the other job	28	54	32
Personal or family reasons	8	9	2
Training	3	<1	0
Other	13	9	4
sample n	**193**	**55**	**44**

In England, the main reason for men and managers moving was reorganisation, in Scotland and Northern Ireland, this most often applied to residential workers. Black staff were more likely than white staff to have changed jobs through reorganisation, and were less likely to say they had left because of the attractions of another job. This was partly due to the concentration of black staff in three English departments, two of which were carrying out internal reorganisation between the interviews. The second most common reason given by each job type was the attraction of another job, particularly by managers and field social work staff in Scotland and Northern Ireland, and residential workers in England. Dissatisfaction was only given as a reason by a minority of staff, although a quarter of field social work staff cited this, as did a third of Northern Ireland residential workers. Twice as many Scottish staff as in the other samples gave dissatisfaction as the main reason for moving, but this still applied only to a minority. Dissatisfaction mainly concerned feelings about the work, lack of career progress and personal development, and the culture and values of the workplace.

As with staff who had applied for another job, mean GHQ12 scores were higher at the first interview for those who subsequently changed jobs, suggesting that the job changing process itself may be stressful for some staff.

Staff who left

Allowing for the differences in time between interviews, broadly similar proportions of staff left each sample. Details are not known of all the staff who left because confidential information about reasons for leaving and contact addresses could not be revealed by personnel departments. However, through several mailwaves we obtained sufficient information to carry out telephone interviews with approximately a quarter of former staff, in which they were asked about the circumstances of leaving the job they were in at the first interview, and what they would be doing next.

Staff who took part in the telephone interviews were not necessarily representative of all staff who left in this period, but in terms of gender and ethnic group, the distribution broadly reflected their representation at the first interview. The main difference was that, mainly as a result of staff who retired, a higher proportion were aged over 50. This was most apparent for staff who left home care jobs in England, four fifths of whom were in this older age group.

As with staff who had changed jobs within the same employing authority, most leavers felt they had chosen this move, but because of the wider range of activities to which they moved, reasons for leaving were more varied. Managers who left mainly did so because of reorganisation or the attractions of another job, and, unlike those who changed jobs within their employing authority, some left because of redundancy, early retirement and personal reasons. Over half gave dissatisfaction as the main or secondary reason for leaving, but since most moved to social care jobs in social services departments outside the scope of the survey, or to independent private or voluntary organisations, this suggests a commitment to a chosen career in social care, in spite of the dissatisfying aspects of the job that was left. The few who left social care work altogether did so mainly because of (early) retirement or poor health.

Field social work staff had mostly been attracted by another job, although over half mentioned dissatisfaction with various aspects of the work as the main or secondary reason. Most moved to other social care work, mainly for another social services department or Board.

Most home care workers who left had reached retirement age or had taken early retirement because of ill-health. Others moved to social care jobs, including home care in other social services departments or Boards, further training or other work, some doing this for personal reasons or through dissatisfaction. Residential workers were similar to home care workers in that most had retired, had taken early retirement on health grounds or had been made redundant. Others left to do qualifying training, or had been attracted by a job in another social services department or

Board, or other social care employer, or had left social care work altogether. A third gave dissatisfaction as one of the reasons for leaving.

Staff have always moved from social services departments into and out of other statutory services, particularly the National Health Service, local authority education welfare services and social work and other teaching in further education colleges and universities (Ginn et al, 1997), and into and out of the independent private and voluntary sectors. Leavers from the Workforce studies moved to each of these employers, mostly from jobs as manager, but also from field social work and residential work. The employers moved to included housing trusts and housing associations, which are increasingly becoming involved in the provision of community care through sheltered housing and residential care; social care and other employment agencies; and national organisations such as Barnardos and the Salvation Army.

The telephone interviews with those who left

About a quarter of staff who left were interviewed by telephone using a semi-structured schedule which encouraged them to describe the circumstances of their departure as fully as they wished. Some gave a very brief account of their leaving, perhaps because they had just one clear cut reason, others gave much more detailed information about the job left and the new post or activity. This is an area in which quantitative data analysis is limited, and although the information gathered was generally associated with job moves, it also gave us some insights into the issues concerning social services staff generally. Dissatisfaction frequently featured as a reason for leaving, and it may be that the semi-structured questions in the telephone interviews encouraged staff to talk about their dissatisfaction, and possibly reconstruct the past. It is also possible that staff who left in less happy circumstances may have been more likely to agree to be interviewed than staff who left for other reasons. Details of the interviews are summarised below, and although not necessarily issues for other staff, we have identified some of the key themes, many of which have been addressed elsewhere in this book, including satisfaction and dissatisfaction, stress, reorganisation and the changing nature of the work.

Dissatisfaction and stress

Just as satisfaction with the present job was the main reason for not applying for another job, dissatisfaction with the present job was one of the main reasons for leaving, particularly for managers and field social work staff, over half of whom expressed dissatisfaction with various aspects of the job. For some staff, dissatisfaction stemmed from personal issues, it being "time to make a change" for one social worker, because, having "done everything several times", the job had lost its challenge. Leaving in this and similar circumstances was a positive move to gain new experience or career advancement.

One of the reasons for leaving given most often was dissatisfaction with the level of stress. For some managers this came from increasing workloads, losing staff, having to supervise extra workers, another team, or another department, and the introduction of "never ending" new procedures, costings and "computerisation". Others were "fed up with 'unsuitable' accommodation", particularly "noisy open plan offices", and felt "dumped on" by "constant" complaints from staff, particularly in the case of some home care managers, who had to deal with changes in staff conditions of employment.

Field social work staff left because of stress from caseloads that were "too big" and having to work too many unofficial hours. Staff shortages made the workload unpredictable and unmanageable, and some duty systems regularly produced court and other work on top of their own caseloads, often requiring very late evening work. Reflecting the perception reported in Chapter Three that paperwork and form filling had increased, stress from the amount of paperwork was the reason for some staff leaving, some feeling that they had to make a written record of "everything" to "cover their backs". For others, working facilities were "inadequate", particularly having to share an office with too many other people.

Some home care workers left because of stress caused by cutbacks in staffing, which in some areas had been so severe that it had become "impossible" to provide the level of service required. There was less time to spend with users and many home care workers felt that the job had become harder and more physically exhausting, and "everything had to be rushed".

Staff in all four job types referred to stress associated with working with some service users. Even in "better" authorities with good training, support and caseload management, child protection work was extremely stressful, partly because it took "too much time to achieve anything", and in the case of one manager, was personally distressing after her own child was born. Changes in community care led to users staying in their own homes longer, and being more frail, home care workers were having to do "the work of a district nurse" instead of just helping with cleaning and shopping. This was not always seen as a bad thing because "people are more important than housework", but it required different skills. However, some home care workers felt that users took advantage of them, and one worker eventually resigned because a user had been "treating her like a slave".

Residential workers also felt stress from more demanding or dependent users. Older people admitted to residential care increasingly suffered from dementia, and some mental health hostels were accommodating difficult "young drug users as opposed to relatively compliant middle aged people". As was discussed in Chapter Five, children and adolescents had become "much more difficult, abusive and dangerous to work with" and discipline had "gone out of the window". Previously "children would never have struck a member of staff", but now staff were regularly "bruised, spat at, bitten and kicked", and often had to "stay up half the night dealing with some kind of trouble". One woman felt that violence was getting worse because staff had so many restrictions placed on them, particularly with rules governing physical contact.

Given the nature of the work, a certain level of stress is inevitable, and as discussed in Chapter Four, this may be alleviated by effective support and supervision. For some leavers, the low level and poor quality of support had contributed to their decision to change jobs. Some managers felt there was a lack of support from higher management in dealing with unprofessional behaviour by supervisees, others felt that the team was unsupportive, staff were unwilling to be flexible, "work hard", or adapt to and learn about the changing needs of users. As in another study by Echtle and Pahl (1992), dissatisfaction with management and supervision was part of the decision to change jobs. One social worker felt able to handle the pressure of work, but left because of the lack of support and the:

> ... **total lack of management, with a high turnover of managers [which resulted in] discontinuity. The team manager was totally inaccessible, was never there and was not helpful when he was there. [There were] very few team meetings, no planning.**

One social worker had wanted to discuss the pressure of work but was told by her manager that "she should know what the job was like" since she had been "doing it for so long"; another social worker felt that the new team leader, an occupational therapist who had been appointed to coordinate different disciplines, had "no understanding" of social work practice.

Dissonance

Some staff decided to leave because there was a mismatch between their expectations and the day to day reality of the job. This was often perceived as being due to the work having changed, particularly some aspects of practice. Some field social work staff felt that child protection work was less satisfying with a shift in emphasis from preventative work to crisis management, others felt that they were not fully using their skills in direct work with users because of increased time spent on office procedures (see also Chapter Three). Some home care managers had seen themselves as "carers", however, but with the "massive" increase in paperwork following the introduction of the community care legislation involving them in financial planning and purchasing services from independent providers, they were left little time to assess users' needs and "get out of the office to support the staff".

Some home care workers felt that the more satisfying aspects of the work were being lost, the job was less personal and much of the close, caring and confiding interaction with users was gone. Working used to be on a one to one basis, now workers would sometimes go in pairs. Residential workers also felt a conflict between their perceptions of themselves as skilled "hands on" workers, when current regulations prevented them from "physically comforting a crying child in private" because of the "potential for accusations of sexual harassment" (sic). An extreme example of this was the case of a residential worker who was dismissed after a lifetime in the job. During an investigation of allegations of sexual abuse made against another worker, a complaint had been made against him for giving a child "a clip around the ear" 20 years ago. This practice was common then, but he had subsequently realised it was wrong and had not repeated it. He felt that he would never be able to work in social care again because he had been judged by current standards which did not allow for the cultural change that had taken place in acceptable standards of practice.

Other sources of dissatisfaction

Negative feelings were expressed about career opportunities in social services, some managers feeling that local authorities as employers were too rigid, lacking in career opportunities outside management, lacking the potential to gain different experience without moving to another job. In the opinion of one manager, unfair recruitment processes contributed to this, particularly equal opportunities policies which did not prevent favouritism and resulted in people "not just (being) protected, but cosseted". One manager left because he felt that his training section was a "cul-de-sac", a community care manager had taken up the first offer of another job because she had felt "trapped" with "no prospect of ever being able to move" because she was "neither experienced nor qualified in anything else". Others disliked the management role, the lack of contact with users, "heavy management decision making" and putting pressure on overworked social workers.

Staff also left because they were dissatisfied with low pay, through which they felt they were not valued; the inaccessibility of training, especially for staff on fixed contracts or with caring responsibilities for their own children; and the lack of recognition of life experience, and experience gained in other work (see also Chapter Seven).

Reorganisation, redeployment and early retirement

As with changing jobs within the same department, reorganisation was most frequently cited as contributing to the decision to leave, either for another job or to take early retirement. Reorganisation affected staff in different ways. Some had to re-apply for their own, a similar or replacement job, sometimes in competition with former colleagues. Some were not reappointed, others were offered unsuitable redeployment. For example, an assistant officer in charge was offered part time work as a care assistant, and a policy coordinator was offered a job as a home care organiser. Some home care workers left after being offered new contracts which introduced unsocial hours, others accepted redundancy, although one home care manager who had "taken the money and run", had received a financial package that was not as good as she had thought.

Some residential establishments were closed down or taken over by housing trusts or housing associations, with some staff staying on with the new employer, but subsequently leaving when they became disillusioned with the new regime. One manager left because he doubted the viability of his authority's plans to set up his day centre as a self supporting independent organisation with the existing staff.

There were staff whose jobs were affected by other consequences of reorganisation. One manager left after her team was outposted to an office where, as the only senior staff member, she felt isolated from other managers, and had much further to commute to work. Talk of reorganisation and redundancies had made one manager apply for another job in spite of being happy with the work, another:

> ... couldn't bear it any longer, [the] very depressed environment, the whole ... section [was] under constant threat of privatisation, cuts and reorganisation, staff morale in the whole of social services was rock bottom ... [through] being bombarded by changes.

Attractions of another job or activity

In spite of the level of dissatisfaction, the perceived attraction of another job was one of the main reasons given for leaving. Some social work staff felt that their new job would provide an opportunity to gain more or different experience, for example, of therapeutic work, or to work with different users. Specialising in a particular area was very attractive, especially social work lecturing, fostering and adoption and work with adults with disabilities or people with HIV disease. Specialisation was not only attractive as a career move or as an opportunity to develop an expertise, it was also seen as a way to reduce stress by making the work more "manageable and predictable", minimising "unplanned overtime and crisis work". Jobs in different work settings were also attractive; being the social work specialist in a multi-disciplinary team was more satisfying for one social worker than being in a specialist team of mental health social workers, and jobs in different locations, such as a county council, were attractive because the users were thought to be "much less dangerous" than in inner London.

Doing the DipSW was attractive to some residential workers as "a way out of residential work". One worker who had left without waiting another year to try again for secondment was finding the placements on his DipSW course, organising community care for older people, much more challenging than residential work, and he planned to get a job in this field when he qualified. Another residential worker had decided to do a degree course in social sciences and social work on a grant so as not to be restricted in her future career. Moving from temporary work for the 'care bank staff' to permanent residential work was also attractive because it was seen as a career move, as was moving from home care to residential work.

Moving to jobs in the independent private and voluntary social care sector

Some leavers saw very positive advantages in moving to jobs outside social services. Other statutory or independent organisations were considered to be less stressful generally; any stress was of a different and more manageable nature, with less red tape and less "complex bureaucracy". For similar pay, a former social work manager felt that there was "less responsibility and less potential for things to go wrong" in the education welfare service: "somebody might die if domiciliary care had not been organised or a worker had failed to turn up, but it is not so serious if somebody does not go to school."

Another manager found his new voluntary organisation: "more optimistic and cheerful due to its independence and being a smaller organisation – nice building, nice work, nice people, things go well as long as contracts [are] met."

Short contracts and freelance employment with independent organisations and specialist social care employment agencies gave some former managers greater variety, including basic grade and "practical" jobs, the main advantage of which was "not having to take work home". This freedom offered "a different way of life" to one manager, although it was only made possible because he was able to supplement the erratic pay from his new work with a pension from his former local authority.

Other favourable consequences of moving to a voluntary agency included being employed on a higher grade, better pay, flexible hours, more annual leave, a non-contributory pension scheme; sponsorship to do qualifying training; "plenty of ideas and energy with a shared vision and ethos amongst staff, an exciting and dynamic problem solving culture"; preventative work being seen as more constructive than child protection work in local authorities; feeling valued and supported; and having more staff development and other training.

However, staff discovered that there were also problems working for the independent sector. Voluntary organisations were less well resourced and there was greater uncertainty over future funding and job security. They were often national organisations without local offices and staff sometimes had to travel long distances to attend meetings, some felt isolated from their colleagues, left to their own devices and unsupported. One officer in charge felt that supervision as understood in local authorities was not available in housing associations:

In local authorities, support and supervision were regular and were provided by people who were experienced or trained to give it. In the voluntary sector, supervision has not been so consistent, the structures aren't there, and on some occasions the support has been the opposite, negative and unhelpful. The individuals providing support do not have the necessary understanding of how to do this, and although we have discussed it, my supervisor says there's nothing wrong with it, and we'll have to agree to differ.

While pay had improved for some managers and field social work staff, in the opinion of one manager, poor pay for basic grade and support staff resulted in a lower calibre of worker which affected the quality of service:

Private and voluntary agencies are now getting the experience of providing home care, but the service is not up to standard because they cut costs and wages to make a profit. Social services home helps are not perfect, but at least they have proper procedures, training and opportunities for [staff] development and promotion.

One residential manager decided to take early retirement after the residential home had been taken over by a voluntary organisation because: "the new manager was sexist, and there was no avenue available to complain about his behaviour. The new hierarchy were all heavy smokers, whereas previously there had been a no smoking policy."

Although independent organisations had less bureaucracy, local authority type bureaucracy was gradually creeping in as former local authority staff were recruited. However, a community care manager felt this was not entirely a bad thing because, although procedures had been simpler, the lack of rules had caused confusion and uncertainty. Some staff found the work in independent organisations "a bit on the periphery of service provision", "missed the adrenaline" and the excitement of the "cutting edge" of service delivery.

Finally, for some staff, leaving social care work was attractive. One care assistant had originally taken the job because it had fitted in with her family life, but had decided to return to her original area of work, in catering, which she preferred, although she had enjoyed the work and felt she had done some good. For one worker, the experience gained in social services had enabled her to get a job in court work without having legal training, an area of work she had always aspired to.

Personal and health reasons

Staff in all four job types who had been happy with the work had to leave for personal reasons. These were mostly connected with family and other commitments, such as maternity leave, moving when a husband, wife or partner had been offered a job elsewhere, or moving from an isolated rural area. Some women gave up full-time work to care for children or elderly parents, or because of difficulties finding childminders due to shift work. Others, particularly home care and residential workers, gave up paid caring work to do unpaid caring work, looking after relatives or their own children or grandchildren. Leavers also moved to jobs closer to home because commuting was too difficult or because the workplace had been relocated. Others wanted to move to a different part of the country, away from inner London, to be able to afford a house with a garden. More time for other interests when she no longer had the financial pressure after her children had left home prompted one manager to take up a part-time job, and another social worker decided to take up six month locum posts which enabled him to save enough money to travel and work abroad in the other six months.

Poor health resulted in some staff having to leave. This particularly affected home care and residential workers, who retired early because of back injuries sustained at work, injuries from road accidents, high blood pressure, or asthma.

Conclusions

This chapter has covered some of the reasons associated with job change among social services staff. It has highlighted the fact that staff who wish to leave or who actually do leave their jobs, are only a minority. At the first interview, a third had planned to change jobs. In the year before the second interview, a fifth had applied for another job, and by the second interview between a fifth and two fifths had been appointed to a new job with the same employer. Although it is difficult to draw direct comparisons with other workforces, these proportions were broadly in line with other studies, particularly nurses in the National Health Service (Seccombe and Smith, 1997).

Historically, most past movement by social services staff was between social care jobs, mostly between jobs of the same type and for the same employer (Ginn et al, 1997), and this pattern continued into the period examined in the Workforce studies. Staff who changed jobs in the past were more likely to do so because of the attraction of another job, but towards the most recent period, reorganisation had become increasingly important as the reason for changing jobs (Ginn et al, 1997), and for staff in England and Northern Ireland, reorganisation had become the most often cited reason for changing jobs within the same employing authority.

Although not representative of all staff who left, the moves made by telephone interviewees were very broadly similar to desired moves by job applicants, and job changes by staff who stayed with the same employer. They made one of four moves: the majority to a job in another social services department or Board; and minorities to social care work in the independent sector or another statutory service; leaving work through retirement, poor health or redundancy; and moving to another activity outside social care. Many reasons were predictable – career moves, personal reasons, retirement – but what was perhaps unexpected was the level of dissatisfaction and amount of stress reported. This would seem to reinforce the findings of other research which has shown that the decision to change jobs is often the final stage in a gradual process of a deteriorating commitment to the work and declining job satisfaction (Knapp et al, 1981). Staff who changed jobs had higher GHQ12 scores at the first interview, indicating a higher level of stress, which was particularly notable in the case of home care workers, the job type least likely to be associated with stress. Nevertheless, although men, younger staff, managers and field social work staff were more likely to change jobs, and were more likely to experience lower satisfaction and higher stress, it has to be remembered that not all staff in these categories changed jobs or experienced low satisfaction or stress. In addition, very few staff left social care work, indicating that dissatisfaction may have been associated with particular jobs, not the work.

Differences between managers and field social work staff and home care and residential workers were quite explicit. Managers and field social work staff moved to another job often with promotion; home care and residential workers more often left for health reasons, to take early retirement, and only rarely moved to another job or made a move that might be regarded as career progression. Differences between job types were of course partly a reflection of the age profile of the workers in each, but the inference is that changing jobs is relatively easy for staff who are well qualified. Thus managers and field social work staff were able to deal with dissatisfaction by leaving, while it may be that because of a lack of opportunities, home care and residential workers who are dissatisfied are unable to leave unless they are entitled to early retirement. Although it could be argued that these were the least likely staff to be dissatisfied, it is important to note the extent to which home care workers felt that the work had become more demanding, with less time to spend with users and the loss of the close confiding relationship with them. Research has clearly shown the importance of the relationship with users as a source of satisfaction (Bartoldus et al, 1989; McLean, 1994) and Chapter Four demonstrated the importance of the link between high job satisfaction and reduced stress. It is also important to bear in mind that residential workers experienced the highest levels of physical and verbal abuse, that residential staff perceived that violence and disruptive behaviour were increasing and that they had a reduced ability to deal with it (see also Chapter Five).

In the light of recent policy to encourage the growth of independent service providers, the comments on working in private and voluntary organisations are extremely enlightening. As with the recruitment of staff from the NHS by private medical services, non-statutory social care providers will increasingly recruit staff formerly employed and trained by social services. The comments about low pay, poor access to training the inferior quality of the service and 'creeping bureaucracy' indicate that in the eyes of some of this group of leavers, there are problems in the independent sector for both service users and staff.

Generally, staff leaving jobs are not lost to the workforce. They take their skills with them and add these to the general pool of knowledge in social services and social care, introducing new enthusiasm and new ways of approaching old problems (Knapp et al, 1981). Regardless of the reasons for changing jobs, most of the skills, knowledge and expertise gained by staff was retained by the same social services department or Board, or within the wider social care field.

TEN

Conclusions and policy issues

Susan Balloch, Mike Fisher and John McLean

Introduction

In the first chapter we voiced concern that research into the social services workforce was neglected in the 1980s and early 1990s. Although the social services expanded during this period, the public debate about welfare was dominated by the attempt to restrict welfare spending and to undermine those working in welfare as 'do-gooders' or as incompetent, more devoted to their own welfare than to that of service users. This is a complex debate, since it intertwines the consumerist approach of the Conservative administrations with the rise of user-led and user-controlled services. On the one hand, social welfare staff, and social workers in particular, certainly deserved the challenge from service users to re-orient their expertise towards assisting the achievement of user-defined rather than professionally-defined goals, resulting in the emphasis on partnership with children and families and on needs-led assessment in community care. On the other hand, government emphasised the common sense nature of much practice in social care, devaluing professional education and training and opening the door to privatising social care services and to reducing the skills and knowledge required for complex tasks, such as community care assessments. This was evidenced in the refusal to extend social work qualifying programmes to three years, and in the removal of probation education and training from social work programmes. Most famously, the then Minister's recommendation following the 'Pindown' affair was that social services should recruit more 'street-wise grannies', and the review by Sir Roy Griffiths of skills required for practice in community care concluded that "there may in fact be a tendency to over-elaborate, both as to the professional input and training required" (DoH, 1988, para 35). Thus the government approach combined with the user movement's demands to produce a highly negative effect on the self-esteem of staff working in social care, an issue emphasised by the views of our sample on whether their work was publicly valued (Balloch et al, 1995).

The political ambivalence towards social services continued into the last election, with no party giving it prominence in the election campaign (Balloch, 1998). Under the Labour government social services have continued to appear peripheral to plans for welfare reform, with the primary focus on public health, education and full employment through the 'New Deal'. Here one can detect aspects of the thinking which dominated Beveridge's reforms in the 1940s, in which the need for social services was expected to diminish in a more prosperous society. The twists and turns of the last 50 years have shown the flaws in this approach, with increasing need for specialist social services brought about not just by rising unemployment but also by changes in family structures and an ageing population. While supporting the need to restructure social services so that they work in closer partnership with service users, and with other agencies essential to care such as health, education and housing, we would argue that demand for effective social services is as great as ever and is unlikely to decrease in the foreseeable future.

Therefore, in the light of our research findings, we will attempt to review in this final chapter the capacity of the workforce to deliver welfare into the next millennium, and to identify what policies would support the workforce to fulfil its role as the key ingredient in high quality, personal social services. We will draw on both the longitudinal elements of the research, showing trends in the findings between the two interviews conducted in 1993-94 and 1995-96, and on the comparability of the findings between the three studies in England, Scotland and Northern Ireland.

The state of the social services workforce

In the statutory sector the social services workforce shares similar conditions of employment, job content, training and qualification patterns. There are, however, also distinct differences between job types, particularly between the office-based job types of manager and field social work staff and direct care providers, home care workers and residential workers. These differences were to be found in current work experience, responsibilities and tasks, past experience, levels of training and qualification, satisfaction, stress, mobility and particularly in terms of the age, gender and other characteristics of the individuals who carry out the work. These differences were similarly reflected in England, Scotland and Northern Ireland, suggesting that there is a commonly accepted understanding of, for example, who will work in home care and what their job will entail. The differences between job types largely reflected the professional and semi-professional nature of the work of management and field social work staff and the manual nature of the work of home care and residential workers.

Professional jobs imply a high proportion of qualified staff who are mostly employed full time on a monthly salary. The majority of social services staff, however, were part-time, weekly paid, unqualified home care workers or care assistants in residential homes, working on low pay with older people. Only a minority of senior residential workers, mostly in childcare, were employed full-time with monthly salaries. Men were in a minority in each job type, but there were higher proportions among the professional and semi-professional categories while part-time lower paid manual jobs were almost exclusively held by women. Changing jobs was relatively easy for managers and field social work staff and, being generally well qualified, job moves more often involved career progression or promotion. In contrast, home care and residential workers lacked opportunities to change jobs. These differences were not simply a function of any particular employer's policies or local labour markets: they were repeated in each sample, in each of the eleven departments or Boards in the study, and reflected a traditional gendered pattern of employment that had changed little in spite of initiatives such as equal opportunities policies or the 1975 Sex Discrimination Act. Although some staff moved between professional and manual job categories, this was unusual and was often, though not exclusively, associated with gaining relevant experience to apply for qualifying training. In the future we envisage a more adaptable workforce with greater mobility between job types and equal career opportunities for all staff.

In assessing the state of the social services workforce, our findings can be interpreted superficially as both positive and reassuring. In England, the workforce had a turnover rate similar to other comparable professions of about 9%, the average length of employment was 10 years and almost four fifths of staff still worked for the same authority they had originally joined. The majority of staff said they would stay in their current line of work even if financial need was removed. Among some groups of staff (such as home care workers) there was a high degree of job satisfaction. Although our analysis points to lack of career progression for women in social services, the evidence suggested that this arose from indirect discrimination rather than from the denial of the potential contribution women can make in senior positions. There was substantial commitment to and enthusiasm for training, especially among black staff aiming at achieving relevant qualifications.

It might appear, therefore, that we have a relatively stable and committed workforce; that this provides a core asset in the provision of social services, and that minor policy adjustments will suffice to address outstanding issues. In our view, however, this would be to mistake resilience for indestructibility.

Our view is that the trends in our findings show a workforce with a deteriorating capacity either to absorb the existing demands of working in welfare, or to respond positively to further change. The evidence centres on stress, exposure to violence and abuse, responses to the changing nature of the job, progress on equal opportunities, and issues in training.

The first interviews identified high levels of stress as an issue for the workforce, and the second interviews showed that, for some staff, stress had continued to rise. It was highest among managers, who, it might be argued, carry the greatest responsibility to effect change. Stress is of course commonplace: the highest estimates suggest that about 28% of the general population score above the threshold on the GHQ measure. However, the corresponding figure for the social services workforce was over a third at each interview and up to two thirds for some groups. It might be seen as inevitable that those paid by society to address some of its most pressing social problems would be exposed to higher than average levels of stress, and the appropriate response might be seen as providing legislative and procedural clarity, especially in areas of high uncertainty such as child protection. The theory would be that lower stress might result from the clarity provided, for example, by the children's legislation and its associated guidance and training initiatives. Our evidence is, however, that those working with children and families experience a lower sense of control over their work, a lower sense of satisfaction, and higher GHQ scores than staff working with older people, an area which it has been argued lacks legislative and procedural clarity (Law Commission, 1991). This means we must go beyond clarifying the responsibilities of social services staff, and look to measures which address the relationship between stress, autonomy and job satisfaction (see Chapter Four).

Compared with other community-based health care workers, such as general practitioners or community nurses, social services staff in our three studies were at much greater risk of being physically attacked. Field social work staff were twice as likely as community psychiatric nurses to experience physical attack in the course of a year, and residential workers were at six times the risk. Although some progress had been made between the two interviews in improving support for staff, it remained true at second interview that over a quarter of managers, a fifth of field social work staff and a quarter of residential workers thought they received a lot less help than necessary in dealing with the effects of violence. Physical violence against social services staff has a wide range of origins, but explanations include the possibility that it denotes a breakdown in consensus about the very basis of welfare between those providing the service and those receiving it. Much training for welfare and staff motivation for work in this field is rooted in notions of a consensus welfare state where those in need are assisted through collective action, and where all share some common idea of rights and responsibilities. The reality is that social services staff work increasingly at the boundaries where the limits of society's obligation to care and the agreed criteria for intervening are being redrawn. The threatening aspect of physical violence is not just the direct risks, but also the implication that a core aspiration of social welfare practice is being undermined. Measures to address violence and abuse towards social services staff must therefore go beyond merely reducing the risks of injury, and must look at the implications for the changing relationship between service users and providers and for staff morale.

Changes in the nature of work are of course inevitable, and many are positive in the sense that they offer new opportunities and growth. The findings show that the workforce experienced a great deal of change, but much of it outside its control. For example, we reported in Chapter Nine that in England over two fifths of those who had moved jobs at the second interview cited reorganisation as the main reason, regardless of their career aspirations expressed two years previously. Perhaps even more important were the changes consequent on the restructuring of welfare, with over two thirds of managers and field social work staff reporting that different demands had affected their work, and that departmental restructuring to implement community care legislation had affected their organisation. Some of this will of course be positive and welcome, but it is unlikely that those staff who at second interview reported spending more time report writing, filling out forms, or coping with reduced staffing (see Chapter Three) regarded these changes as beneficial, either to the service or to themselves. Other studies of community care show staff unsure about the core of their practice and worried that their skills, knowledge and values were no longer appreciated (for example, Lewis and Glennerster, 1996; Levin and Webb, 1997). We highlighted in our first report the importance of a sense of helping people in sustaining job satisfaction, and the frustration caused if staff found the work environment interfering with this (Balloch et al, 1995; Chapter Four). Our point is that if the core of the job changes beyond what members of the workforce see as compatible with their goals and values, the resulting dissonance will be costly in terms of the quality of the service and will hinder further policy change.

Progress on equal opportunities is vital in services which aim to base their work on notions of empowerment and equity. If staff do not experience their organisations as fulfilling equal opportunities policies, it is difficult to see how they can pursue these goals with service users. At a very practical level, for example, the success of agencies in addressing the importance of gender in shaping the lives and needs of service users will be enhanced if similar recognition characterises their employment policies. Although the responsibility to reshape services to meet the needs of minority ethnic groups is shared by all social services staff, it will be more successfully undertaken if black staff are in a position to make a significant contribution. Our findings showed a lack of progress in addressing key issues in equal opportunities, and, in relation to racial equality, substantially discordant perceptions between black and white staff. In contrast, community identification was not an issue causing significant division between staff in Northern Ireland.

The position of black staff continues to cause concern (Chapter Six). In a one year period, four out of 10 black staff in England reported racism from service users or relatives, and over a quarter experienced racism from colleagues. The majority of black staff experiencing racism felt they had not received adequate support from their department. Black staff were unconvinced of the effectiveness of their department's equal opportunities policies, unlike their white colleagues, who were much more positive about their implementation. Racism is of course a widespread, divisive force in society, and its reduction in the working experiences of black staff in social services would not preclude its influence on other aspects of their lives. Nevertheless, the extent to which black staff are exposed to racism, particularly from colleagues, leads to legitimate questions about whether its effects on staff and on the quality of service are given sufficient priority by social services managers, and whether an organisation inadequately dealing with its internal sources of racism can successfully address it in the lives of service users.

Training has traditionally provided some of the answers to social services organisations facing immense change, and our findings (Chapter Eight) show the enormous energy and resources devoted to training, and the high degree of interest among staff in improving skills and knowledge through training. There remain, however, significant problems in securing a continuum of training, from NVQs/SVQs through to the DipSW, PQ and Advanced Award levels. The low take up of NVQ/SVQ training is especially worrying: this training is often aimed at staff working in home care, and, as the nature of their work changes in response to the continuing care responsibilities increasingly adopted by social services, skill change and renewal is vital. At a period when mobility between jobs within the service is essential, there was evidence that those who changed jobs did not, in their view, receive sufficient training for the change of responsibility. Additionally, over the 12 months prior to the second interview one in four staff reported they were unable to obtain training they sought. A majority of staff qualified in social work did so in the 1970s and 1980s, prior to the major changes consequent on children's legislation and the new arrangements for community care. Skill renewal is thus at a premium among qualified staff, in the context where there is little research evidence from in-service training pointing to successful ways of modifying their performance. The evidence about preferred learning styles is a further cause for concern: relying on life experience or more experienced colleagues are essentially strategies for conserving and maximising existing knowledge and skills, rather than strategies for re-examining the fundamental basis for the practice of welfare implied in the restructuring of services and sought by user groups. Overall, this picture suggests that the workforce is not re-skilling at a rate commensurate with the pace of change, and not re-thinking the place of skills and knowledge gained from life experience within the wider framework of responsive, consumer-oriented services.

It is not yet clear how the separate National Training Organisations being set up in England, Scotland, Northern Ireland and Wales by TOPSS, the Training Organisation for the Personal Social Services, will address these problems. Their policies will inevitably be more strongly influenced by the training needs identified by employers than by those selected by the staff themselves and service users, or by the longer term need for a flexible, well-educated workforce. In England one focus will certainly be on a redistribution of the training support programme grant, currently controlled by the local authorities, across statutory, voluntary and private sectors. Unless further funds can be found for training, from, for example, Training and Enterprise Councils, funding to the statutory sector will be reduced. However, with a substantial proportion of available training funds earmarked for young adults under 25, the social services workforce with an average age of over 30 may lose out.

The competing demands of work and home significantly affect social care staff. A much higher proportion of social services staff were carers than in the general population in employment and their levels of stress were higher than for other staff (Balloch et al, 1997). If women, they were more likely to work part-time, with adverse consequences for their career progression, and the skills and knowledge acquired in this role were unlikely to be valued. The extent of caring responsibility among social services staff is a new finding, and addressing it will require far more 'family friendly policies' than hitherto have prevailed. It is reasonable to think that social services' work with carers will benefit in quality and relevance if the needs of staff who themselves are carers are recognised.

Equal opportunities for women continues to be an issue in social services. As stated earlier, women continue to be under-represented in senior management in social services, despite almost a decade of action. The new elements in our research findings are, firstly, that we show (in Chapter Seven) that women in social work are as motivated and committed as men, and secondly, that discrimination against women is indirect, in the sense that it is a consequence of women's lower level of qualification, shorter full-time service, and of the organisation's undervaluing the life-skills they bring to their work. The importance of these findings is that they are all capable of remedy by determined management, supported by national strategy.

Continuity and change

Our theme has been about continuity and change. The change of government in 1997 raised questions about new policy towards social services to which the 1998 White Paper responded positively (Secretary of State 1998, Cm 4169) though new arrangements for inspection and regulation will not be implemented until well into the new century. So far continued support for previous spending plans has meant continuity, at least in terms of close central control over spending on local authority services and social security. Although the previous requirement to spend 85% of social care funding on independent care provision has been rescinded, and replaced with an emphasis on 'Best Value', voluntary and private provision of social care services continues to grow. This means that social care employment will increasingly be located in the voluntary and private care sectors. If the intention is to relocate existing staff, our evidence is that very few have past experience of working in social care outside the statutory sector, so the majority of the workforce would not have prior experience to call upon. Moreover, few staff would, on our evidence, choose such a move. When asked about their career plans, the majority thought it likely they would remain in statutory social services and unlikely they would move to the voluntary or private sector. The intended further growth of voluntary and private sector care provision may therefore be hindered by a workforce reluctant to transfer employment.

If staff are forced to move out of the statutory sector, will they lose their motivation and commitment to work? Lack of that commitment, so evident in the statutory workforce of the past, may lead not only to dissatisfaction among staff, but also to a reduction in the quality of services they provide. Recent studies of other workforces show the importance of what is termed affective commitment (see also Chapter Eight) in allowing organisations to fulfil their goals effectively (Meyer and Allen, 1997). Affective commitment is what motivates staff to 'go the extra mile' to provide service users with good service because of a conviction that this is what the organisation is about. It is the motivation that lies behind the majority of social services staff who say that even if they were comfortably off, they would wish to continue their work in social services.

This analysis is clearly relevant to our findings on certain groups of staff whose work includes experiences which might compound disaffection. Black staff who experience racism or who perceive that the organisation does not adequately pursue equal opportunities policies, or women who feel that their skills and experiences are less highly valued, are highly likely to question the fit between personal and organisational goals. Studies of the concept of inclusion at work confirm the importance of this line of analysis. In exploring the experiences of minority groups in employment, Mor-Barak and her colleagues have underlined the importance of a sense of feeling included at work, defined as access to information and resources, involvement in work groups and the ability to influence decision making (Mor-Barak and Cherin, 1998). In the Workforce studies only a third of managers and field social work staff were satisfied with the amount of influence they had and this was one of the least satisfying aspects of the work for home care and residential workers. Mor-Barak and Cherin warn that "employees' behaviours are based to a significant degree on their perception of their inclusion or exclusion in the social system" and that "the degree to which this desire to belong is accommodated by the organisation potentially affects employee job satisfaction and organisational commitment" (1998, pp 60-1).

These wider perspectives on the role of commitment and inclusiveness in organisations indicate the important influence of workforce attitudes and feelings on organisational performance. They suggest that quality in services depends in large measure on the attitudes and feelings that members of staff bring to their work and logic suggests the enhanced importance of this approach when the product is welfare, achieved through the relationship that service providers make with service users. In turn this suggests the need for a comprehensive human resources strategy for social care which recognises the key role played by the workforce in providing quality services.

In the future it is also likely that more and more social work and social care staff will find themselves working, not only in the non-statutory sector, but in other settings such as primary care, schools, community development agencies and housing agencies, with which they have previously been unfamiliar and in which specific support for their work may be lacking. A way has to be found, therefore, to sustain the outstanding commitment that social services staff in the statutory sector have demonstrated while facilitating their adaptation to the new working situations and realities of the twenty-first century. Training may provide a partial solution, professional and trades union organisations another, although union membership is not well developed in the voluntary and private sectors.

The government's intention to establish the General Social Care Council (GSCC) has indicated a readiness to look at new ways of addressing the relationship between the public need for confidence in social care staff and the sector's need for clarity about eligibility to work in social care. It is arguable that, in part, the GSCC represents a logical continuation of the distrust of public welfare officials evidenced in previous governments' policies and stemming ultimately from the conviction that public officials are motivated primarily by self-interest rather than by commitment to welfare, 'budget maximisers' rather than public servants (Dunleavy, 1985; Dunleavy and Hood, 1994). We are not arguing here that the public does not need protection in the form of the GSCC proposals for registration, but rather that the prominence of the regulatory approach has to be balanced by an equal emphasis on the workforce as an essential resource.

The Workforce studies do not suggest that further, radical changes may easily be assimilated. Our view is that the workforce is indeed resilient, that it has much to offer social services into the next millennium, including commitment, maturity and experience, but that it is not indestructible. There are limits to the amount of change it can absorb, and our evidence is that, in terms of stress, exposure to violence, inadequate progress on equal opportunities and on training, its ability to implement the core values of a restructured personal social services is being severely stretched.

Moving beyond registration and competence

What is sometimes termed the 'new landscape' of social care certainly opens up possibilities for addressing the problems of providing a skilled, knowledgeable and trustworthy social care workforce. We must, however, go beyond measures to achieve regulation and competence: these will not on their own be enough to generate and maintain an expert and committed workforce. A coherent and comprehensive human resources strategy, valuing the workforce as the primary resource for a restructured social services, requires a new consensus to underpin management and practice, addressing the changing role of social care in the welfare state and the changing knowledge and skills required for effective practice. Achieving this consensus will require dialogue between government, employers, employees and user groups, perhaps under the auspices of the GSCC. We also need to ensure that social services maximise the potential contribution of all members of staff. This will mean placing greater value on women's experiences of caring, their part-time work and their aspirations towards management and finding ways of attracting more men into paid caring roles. At the same time we will need to give higher priority to addressing equal opportunities for black staff in social services, whose contribution risks being impeded by their experience of racism and by lack of support in dealing with it.

Stress and violence are serious occupational hazards and determined steps are required to reduce staff exposure to them, to provide better support and to examine ways of enhancing job satisfaction and a sense of control over work. Last but not least, we must continue to invest in appropriate and coherent education and training for the social services workforce, to enhance levels of qualification, encourage all staff to view training as an integral part of their work and to acknowledge the training needs associated with job change. We also need to provide a continuum of development from vocational qualifications to post-qualifying awards.

Such a programme would provide the basis for renegotiating the commitment of the workforce to a new vision of social welfare in which social services, in partnership with other agencies, act as a force for a more equal, inclusive society.

Bibliography

Alimo-Metcalfe, B. (1991) 'What a waste! Women in the National Health Service', *Women in Management Review and Abstracts*, vol 6, no 5, pp 17-24.

Allen, P. (1982) 'Size of workforce, morale and absenteeism: a re-examination', *British Journal of Industrial Relations*, vol 20, no 1, pp 83-100.

Allen, P., Pahl, J. and Quine, L. (1990) *Care staff in transition*, London: HMSO.

Aye Maung, A. and Mirrlees-Black, C. (1994) *Racially motivated crime: A British crime survey analysis*, London: Home Office.

Bagley, C. and Young, L. (1982) 'Problems of adoption for Black children', in J. Cheetham (ed) *Social work and ethnicity*, London: Allen and Unwin.

Bailey, N., Bowes, A. and Sims, D. (1997) 'The demography of minority ethnic groups in Scotland', in A. Bowes and D. Sims (eds) *Perspectives on welfare, the experience of minority ethnic groups in Scotland*, Aldershot: Ashgate.

Baines, C. (1991) 'The professions and an ethic of care', in C. Baines, P. Evans and S. Neysmith (eds) *Women's caring: Feminist perspectives on social welfare*, Toronto: McClelland and Stewart, pp 36-72.

Balloch, S. (1998) 'New partnerships for social services', in H. Jones and S. MacGregor (eds) *Social issues and party politics*, London and New York: Routledge, pp 106-20.

Balloch, S., Pahl, J. and McLean, J. (1998) 'Working in the social services: job satisfaction, stress and violence', *British Journal of Social Work*, vol 28, no 3, pp 329-50.

Balloch, S., Hume, C., Jones, B. and Westland, P. (1985) *Caring for unemployed people: The impact of unemployment on demand for social services*, London: Bedford Square Press.

Balloch, S., Andrew, T., Ginn, J., McLean, J., Pahl, J. and Williams, J. (1995) *Working in the social services,* London: NISW.

Balloch, S., Andrew, T., Ginn, J., McLean, J., Pahl, J. and Williams, J. (1996) *Working in the social services: A comparison of five local authorities in England,* London: NISW.

Balloch, S., Andrew, T., Davey, B., Dolan, L., Fisher, M., Ginn, J., McLean, J. and Pahl, J. (1997) *The social services workforce in transition,* London: NISW.

Bartoldus, E., Gillery, B. and Sturges, P. (1989) 'Job related stress and coping among home care workers with elderly people', *Health and Social Work,* August, vol 14, no 3, pp 204-10.

Beck, D. (1987) 'Counsellor burnout in family service agencies', *Social Casework: The Journal of Contemporary Social Work,* January, pp 3-15.

Beishon, S., Virdee, S. and Hagell, A. (1995) *Nursing in a multi-ethnic NHS,* London: PSI.

Bhat, A., Carr-Hill, R. and Ohri, S. (eds) (1988) *Britain's Black population,* Aldershot: Gower.

Bibby, P. (1994) *Personal safety for social workers,* Aldershot: Arena.

Bowling, A., Farquar, M., Grundy, E. and Formby, J. (1992) *Psychiatric morbidity among people aged 85+: A follow up study,* London: Age Concern Institute of Gerontology.

Brewer, J. (1991) 'The parallels betwen sectarianism and racism: the Northern Ireland Experience', in CCETSW (ed) *One small step towards racial justice: The teaching of anti-racism in Diploma in social work programmes,* Paper 7, London: CCETSW, pp 96-119.

Brown, C. and Gay, P. (1986) *Racial discrimination: 17 years after the Act,* London: PSI.

Brown, R., Bute, S. and Ford, P. (1986) *Social workers at risk: The prevention and management of violence,* London: Macmillan.

Buck, N., Gershuny, J., Rose, D. and Scott, J. (1994) *Changing households: The British Household Panel Survey 1990–1992,* Colchester: University of Essex.

Buglass, D. (1993) *Assessment and care management: A Scottish overview of impending change*, Community Care in Scotland Discussion Paper, no 2, Social Work Research Centre, University of Stirling.

Buglass, D., Balloch, S., Andrew, T., Davey, B., Dolan, L., Fisher, M., Ginn, J., McLean, J. and Pahl, J. (1998) *A workforce in transition: A study of staff in a social work department in Scotland*, London: NISW.

Butt, J. (1994) *Same service or equal service?*, London: HMSO.

Butt, J. and Davey, B. (1997) 'The experiences of Black staff in the social services', in M. May, E. Brunsden and G. Craig (eds) *Social policy review*, no 9, pp 141-61.

Butt, J. and Mirza, K. (1996) *Social care and Black communities*, London: HMSO.

Butt, J., Gorbach, P. and Ahmad, B. (1994) *Equally fair?*, London: HMSO.

Campanelli, P. and Channell, J. (1994) *Training: An exploration of the word and the concept with an analysis of the implications for survey design*, Research Series no 30, Employment Department.

Care Sector Consortium (1996) *NVQ takeup survey: Care and child care and education awards*, London: LGMB.

Carlisle, D. (1997) 'Wait and see', *Community Care*, 20-26 March, p 12.

CCETSW (1996) *1995 Employment survey of newly qualified social workers*, London: CCETSW.

Collings, J. and Murray, P. (1996) 'Predictors of stress amongst social workers: an empirical study', *British Journal of Social Work*, vol 26, no 3, pp 375-87.

Cooper, C.L., Cooper, R.D. and Eaker, L.H. (1988) *Living with stress*, London: Penguin.

Cournoyer, B. (1988) 'Personal and professional distress among social careworkers', *Social Casework: The Journal of Contemporary Social Work*, May, pp 259-64.

Coyle, A. (1988) 'Continuity and change: women in paid work', in A. Coyle and J. Skinner (eds) *Women and work: Positive action for change*, Basingstoke: Macmillan, pp 1-14.

Coyle, A. and Skinner, J. (eds) (1988) *Women and work: Positive action for change*, Basingstoke: Macmillan.

Crane, D. (1986) *Violence on social workers*, Social Work Monograph 46, Norwich: University of East Anglia.

CRE (Commission for Racial Equality) (1989) *Racial equality in social services departments*, London: CRE.

CRE (1995) *Local authorities and racial equality*, London: CRE.

Crompton, R. and Sanderson, K. (1986) 'Credentials and careers: some implications of the increase in professional qualifications amongst women', *Sociology*, vol 20, pp 25-41.

D'Urso, P. and Hobbs, R. (1989) 'Aggression and the general practitioner', *British Medical Journal*, vol 298, pp 97-8.

Darvill, G. (1996) *Management training: The role of open learning*, Conference Paper, Training Social Services Staff: Evidence From New Research, London.

Davies, C. and Rosser, J. (1986) *Processes of discrimination: A study of women working in the NHS*, London: DHSS.

Davies, M. (1985) *The essential social worker: A guide to positive practice*, Aldershot: Gower Publishing.

Davis, A. (1989) 'Home from home: women and local authority residential care', in C. Hallett (ed) *Women and social services departments*, London: Harvester Wheatsheaf.

Dex, S. (1987) *Women's occupational mobility: A lifetime perspective*, Basingstoke: Macmillan.

Dex, S. (1991) *The reliability of recall data: A literature review*, Working Papers of the ESRC Research Centre on Microsocial Change, Paper 11, Colchester: University of Essex.

Dexter, M. and Harbert, W. (1983) *The home help service*, London: Tavistock.

Dobson, R. (1996) 'Out of isolation', *Community Care*, 26 September, pp 22-3.

DoH (Department of Health) (1988) *Violence to staff: Report of the DHSS advisory committee on violence to staff*, London: HMSO.

DoH (1996a) *Statistical bulletin: Community care statistics, 1995*, London: Government Statistical Service.

DoH (1996b) 'Training by design – SSI inspection of social services departments' planning and review processes relating to the training support programme' London: SSI.

DoH (1998) *Statistical bulletin: Personal Social Services staff of Social Services Department at 30 September 1997, England*, London: Government Statistical Service.

DoH and Social Services (1998) *Fit for the future*, Belfast: DoH and Social Services, Northern Ireland Office.

DoH and Social Services Registrar General Northern Ireland (1992) *The Northern Ireland Census 1991*, Belfast: HMSO.

Dominelli, L. (1996) 'Deprofessionalising social work: anti-oppressive practice, competencies and postmodernism', *British Journal of Social Work*, vol 26, no 2, pp 153-75.

Dunleavy, P. (1985) 'Bureaucrats, budgets and the growth of the state', *British Journal of Political Science*, vol 15, pp 299-328.

Dunleavy, P. and Hood, C. (1994) 'From old public administration to new public management', *Public Money and Management*, July–September, pp 9-16.

Echtle, C. and Pahl, J. (1992) *Expectations and reality: A study of staff in the social services*, London: NISW/Reed Care.

Equal Opportunities Commission (1991) *Equality of management: Women's employment in the NHS*, London: HMSO.

Evetts, J. (1994a) 'Introduction', in J. Evetts (ed) *Women and career: Themes and issues in advanced industrial societies*, Harlow: Longman, pp 1-12.

Evetts, J. (1994b) 'Career and gender: the conceptual challenge', in J. Evetts, (ed) *Women and career: Themes and issues in advanced industrial societies*, Harlow: Longman, pp 223-33.

Fabb, J. and Guthrie, T.G. (1997) *Social work law in Scotland,* 2nd edn, Edinburgh: Butterworths.

Fein, E. and Staff, I. (1991) 'Measuring the use of time', *Administration in Social Work*, vol 15, no 4, pp 81-93.

Fineman, S. (1985) *Social work stress and intervention*, Aldershot: Gower.

Fisher, M. (1997) 'Research, knowledge and practice in community care', *Issues in Social Work Education*, vol 17, no 22, pp 17-30.

Fletcher, B. and Payne, R. (1980) 'Stress and work: a review and a theoretical framework – Part 1', *Personnel Review*, vol 9, no 1, pp 1-20.

Gibson, F., McGrath, A. and Reid, N. (1989) 'Occupational stress in social work', *British Journal of Social Work*, vol 19, no 1, pp 1-18.

Ginn, J. (1996) 'Part time employees: volunteers or pressed women?', *Radical Statistics*, vol 62, pp 26-7.

Ginn, J. (1997) 'Gender differences at work', in S. Balloch, T. Andrew, B. Davey, L. Dolan, M. Fisher, J. Ginn, J. McLean and J. Pahl, *The social services workforce in transition*, London: NISW.

Ginn, J. and Buglass, D. (1996) *Working in social work departments in Scotland: An analysis of work histories*, London: NISW.

Ginn, J. and Sandell, J. (1997) 'Balancing home and employment: stress reported by social services staff', *Work, Employment and Society*, vol 11, no 3, pp 413-34.

Ginn, J., Andrew, T., Balloch, S. and McLean, J. (1997) *Work histories of social services staff*, London: NISW.

Ginn, J., Arber, S., Brannen, J., Dale, A., Dex, S., Elias, P., Moss, P., Pahl, J., Roberts, C. and Rubery, J. (1996) 'Feminist fallacies: a reply to Hakim on women's employment', *British Journal of Sociology*, vol 47, no 1, pp 169-74.

Glover, J. and Arber, S. (1995) 'Polarisation in mothers' employment: occupational class, age of youngest child, employment rights and work hours', *Work, Employment and Society*, vol 2, no 4, pp 165-79.

Goldberg, D. (1972) *The detection of psychiatric illness by questionnaire*, Maudsley monograph no 21, London: Oxford University Press.

Goldberg, D. (1978) *Manual of the general health questionnaire*, Windsor: NFER-Nelson.

Goodenough, A. (1996) *Covering the gaps: A new form of brokerage*, London: CCETSW.

Grimwood, C. and Popplestone, R. (1993) *Women, management and care,* Basingstoke: BASW/Macmillan.

Hakim, C. (1995) 'Five feminist myths about women's employment', *British Journal of Sociology,* vol 46, no 3, pp 429-55.

Hallett, C. (1990) 'The gendered world of the social services department', in C. Hallett (ed) *Women and social services departments,* London: Harvester Wheatsheaf.

Harding, T. and Beresford, P. (1996) *The standards we expect,* London: NISW.

Harris, A. (1989) 'Violence in general practice', *British Medical Journal,* vol 298, pp 63-4.

Haskey, J. (1996) 'The ethnic minority populations of Great Britain: their estimated sizes and age profiles', *Population trends,* London: HMSO.

Hayes, P. and Glastonbury, B. (1989) *Social work in crisis: A study of conditions in six local authorities,* London: NALGO.

Herzberg, F., Mausner, B., Peterson, R.O. and Capwell, D.F. (1957) *Job attitudes: Review of research and opinion,* Pittsburgh: Psychological Service of Pittsburgh.

Hills, D., Child, C., Hills, J. and Blackburn, V. (1997) *Towards qualified leadership of residential child care. Summary report on the evaluation of the residential child care initiative,* London: Evaluation Development and Review Unit, Tavistock Institute.

Hopkins, J. (1996) 'Employers count the cost of an absent workforce', *Professional Social Work,* October, pp 6-7.

Horwath, J. (1996) 'Undertaking a training needs analysis within a social care organisation', in N. Connelly (ed) *Training social services staff: Evidence from new research,* London: NISW.

HSE (Health and Safety Executive) (1975) *Health and safety at work Act: The Act outlined,* London: HMSO.

HSE (1988) *Preventing violence to staff,* London: HMSO.

HSE (1990) *A guide to the Health and Safety at Work Act 1974,* London: HMSO.

HSE (1993) *Prevention of violence to staff in banks and building societies,* London: HMSO.

HSE (1995) *Preventing violence to retail staff*, London: HMSO.

Hughes, L. and Pengelly, P. (1995) 'Who cares if the room is cold? Practicalities, projections and the trainer's authority', in M. Yelloly and M. Henkel (eds) *Learning and teaching in social work: Towards reflective practice*, London: Jessica Kingsley.

Hughes, W.H., Patterson, W.J. and Whalley, H. (1986) *Report of the Committee of Inquiry into Children's Homes and Hostels (the 'Hughes' Report)*, Belfast: HMSO.

Humphries, B. (1997) 'Reading social work: competing discourses in the rules and requirements for the Diploma in Social Work', *The British Journal of Social Work*, vol 27, no 5, pp 641-58.

Itzin, C. and Phillipson, C. (1993) *Age barriers at work: Maximising the potential of mature and older people*, Solihull: Metropolitan Authorities Recruitment Agency.

Jackson, C. and Barber, L. (1993) *Women in the NHS: Experiences in South East Thames*, Brighton: Institute of Manpower Studies.

Jayaratne, S. and Chess, W. (1984) 'Job satisfaction and turnover: a national study', *Social Work*, vol 29, no 5, pp 448-53.

Jones, G. (1989) 'Women in social care: the invisible army', in C. Hallett (ed) *Women and social services departments*, Hemel Hempstead: Harvester Wheatsheaf.

Joseph, M.V. and Conrad, A.P. (1989) 'Social work influence on interdisciplinary ethical decision making in health care settings', *Health and Social Work*, vol 14, no 1, pp 22-30.

Joseph Rowntree Foundation Findings (1995) *Job satisfaction and dissatisfaction amongst residential care workers*, Social Care Research, no 69, June.

Kahan, B. and Levy, A. (1991) *The Pindown experience and the protection of children. Report of the Staffordshire Child Care Inquiry*, Staffordshire County Council.

Karasek, R. (1979) 'Job demands, job decision latitude and mental strain. Implications for job redesign', *Administrative Quarterly*, vol 24, pp 285-308.

Kelly, A. (1991) 'The 'new' managerialism in social services', in P. Carter, T. Jeffs and M. Smith (eds) *Social work and social welfare: Yearbook 3*, Buckingham: Open University Press, pp 178-93.

King, J. (1989) 'How do you handle violence?', *Community Care*, 23 March, pp 22-3.

Kinney, J. (1995) *Violence at work: How to make your company safer for employees and customers*, Englewood Cliffs, NJ: Prentice Hall.

Knapp, M., Harissis, K. and Missiakoulis, S. (1981) 'Who leaves social work', *British Journal of Social Work*, vol 11, no 4, pp 412-44.

Knight, J. (1994) 'Motherhood and management', in M. Tanton (ed) *Women in management: A developing presence*, London: Routledge, pp 141-61.

Landy, F. J. (1989) *Psychology of work behaviour*, 4th edn, Belmont, CA: Wadsworth Inc.

Lane, D. (1994) *An independent review of the residential child care initiative*, London: CCETSW.

Law Commission (1991) *Mentally incapacitated adults and decision-making: An overview*, London: HMSO.

Leadbetter, D. and Trewartha, R. (1996) *Handling aggression and violence at work*, Lyme Regis: RHP.

Levin, E. and Webb, S. (1997) *Social work and community care: Changing roles and tasks*, London: NISW Research Unit.

Lewis, J. and Glennerster, H. (1996) *Implementing the new community care*, Buckingham: Open University Press.

LGMB (Local Government Management Board) (1995) *Social services workforce analysis 1994*, London: LGMB/ADSS.

LGMB (1996) *Social services workforce analysis, 1995 Survey*, London: LGMB.

LGMB (1997a) *Social services workforce analysis main report 1996 Survey*, LGMB/ADSS.

LGMB (1997b) *Independent sector workforce survey 1996*, London: LGMB.

LGMB/CCETSW (1997) *Human resources for the personal social services*, London: LGMB/CCETSW.

Library Association (1987) *Violence in libraries: Issues, policies and procedures*, London: Library Association.

Lindow, V. and Morris, J. (1995) *Service user involvement: Synthesis of findings and experience in the field of community care*, York: Joseph Rowntree Foundation.

Locke, E.A. (1976) 'The nature and causes of job satisfaction', in M.D. Dunnette (ed) *The handbook of industrial and organisational psychology*, Chicago: Rand McNally.

Lyons, K., Valle, I.L. and Grimwood, C. (1995) 'Career patterns of qualified social workers: discussion of a recent survey', *British Journal of Social Work*, vol 25, no 2, pp 173-90.

Macran, S., Dex, S. and Joshi, H. (1996) 'Employment after childbearing: a survival analysis', *Work, Employment and Society*, vol 10, no 2, pp 273-96.

Mansell, J. and Beasley, F. (1993) 'Small staffed homes for people with a severe learning disability and challenging behaviour', *The British Journal of Social Work*, vol 23, no 4, pp 329-44.

Marsh, P. and Triseliotis, J. (1996) *Ready to practise? Social work and probation officers: Their training and first year in work*, Aldershot: Avebury.

Mason, D. and Jewson, N. (1992) 'Race, equal opportunities policies and employment practice: reflections on the 1980s, prospects for the 1990s', *New Community*, vol 19, no 1, pp 99-112.

Mayhew, P., Elliott, D. and Dowds, L. (1989) *The 1988 British Crime Survey*, Home Office Research Study 111, London: HMSO.

Mayhew, P., Maung, N.A. and Mirrlees-Black, C. (1993) *The 1992 British Crime Survey*, Home Office Research Study 132, London: HMSO.

McConkey, W. (1995) *Working in the social services in Northern Ireland*, London: NISW.

McConkey, W. (1998) *The Northern Ireland social services workforce: Qualifications and mobility*, London: NISW.

McConkey, W., Balloch, S., Andrew, T., Davey, B., Dolan, L., Fisher, M., Ginn, J., McLean, J. and Pahl, J. (1997) *The Northern Ireland social services workforce in transition*, London: NISW.

McDonald, C., Lyon, C. and George, C. (1990) *Equalling the opportunity: Survey of staff in three Scottish regions*, Stirling: Central Regional Council.

McDougall, M. (1996) 'Using human resource development to progress women into management', in S. Briley (ed) *Women in the workforce: Human resource development strategies into the next century*, Edinburgh: HMSO, pp 14–22.

McKeganey, N. (1989) 'The role of home help organisers', *Social Policy and Administration*, vol 23, no 2, pp 171–8.

McLean, J. (1994) 'Coping with caring', *Care Weekly*, 21 July, p 9.

McLean, J. (1995) 'The experience of working in the social services', in S. Balloch, T. Andrew, J. Ginn, J. McLean, J. Pahl and J. Williams (eds) *Working in the social services*, London: NISW, pp 57–96.

McLean, J. and Andrew, T. (1998) *Residential workers and qualifying training: A preliminary investigation into the careers of residential workers who become qualified*, London: NISW.

Meyer, J. and Allen, N. (1997) *Commitment in the workplace: Theory, research and application*, London: Sage.

Mor-Barak, M. and Cherin, D. (1998) 'A tool to expand organizational understanding of workforce diversity: developing a measure of inclusion-exclusion', *Administration in Social Work*, vol 22, no 1, pp 47–64.

Murray, C. (1997) 'Gender inequality in social work management: cause for pessimism or signs of progress?', in L. Keeble and M. Fisher (eds) *Making a difference: Women and career progression in social services*, London: NISW, pp 25–38.

Newman, J. and Clarke, J. (1994) 'Going about our business? The managerialisation of public services', in J. Clarke, A. Cochrane and E. McLaughlin (eds) *Managing social policy*, London: Sage, pp 13–31.

Nicholson, N., Brown, C. and Chadwick-Jones, J. (1976) 'Absence from work and job satisfaction', *Journal of Applied Psychology*, vol 61, pp 106–8.

NISW (National Institute for Social Work) (1982) *Social workers their role and tasks* (The Barclay Report), London: Bedford Square Press.

Nixon, J. (1993) 'Implementation in the hands of senior managers: community care in Britain', in M. Hill (ed) *New agendas in the study of policy processes*, Hemel Hempstead: Harvester, pp 197-216.

Norris, D. with Kedward, C. (1990) *Violence against social workers: The implications for practice*, London: Jessica Kingsley Publishers.

Norris, P. (1995) *Stress in the workforce and absenteeism*, Conference Paper, 'A force for the future: researching and planning the social services workforce', London, 24 April.

North, S.J. (1996) 'Stress: counselling services', *Community Care,* 31 October-6 November, pp 20-1.

O'Leary, R. (1990) *Report on social work education provision in response to the needs of social workers, educationalists and the minority ethnic communities in Northern Ireland*, Belfast: Bryson House.

ONS (Office of National Statistics) (1997) *Labour force survey*, London: The Stationery Office.

Owens, S. and Keville, H. (1990) *Safe and secure: How to deal with potential violence at work*, St Leonards-on-Sea: Outset Publishing.

Payne, M. (1995) *Social work and community care*, London: Macmillan.

Payne, R.L. (1979) 'Demands, supports, constraints, and psychological health', in C.J. Mackay and T. Cox (eds) *Response to stress: Occupational aspects*, London: International Publishing Corporation.

Phillips, C., Stockdale, J. and Joeman, L. (1989) *The risks of going to work*, London: Suzy Lamplugh Trust.

Pollitt, C. (1993) *Managerialism and the public services: The Anglo-American experience*, Oxford: Blackwell.

Qureshi, H. and Pahl, J. (1992) *Research on the social services workforce*, London: NISW.

Rai, D.K. (1994) *Developments in training in social services*, London: NISW.

Rizzo, J., House, R. and Lirtzman, S. (1970) 'Role conflict and ambiguity in complex organisations', *Administrative Science Quarterly,* vol 15, pp 150-63.

Ross, E. (1993) 'Preventing burnout among social workers in the field of AIDS/HIV', *Social Work in Health care*, vol 18, no 2, pp 91-108.

Rowett, C. (1986) *Violence in social work*, Cambridge: Cambridge Institute of Criminology.

Rowett, C. and Breakwell, G. (1992) *Managing violence at work, course leader's guide*, Windsor: NFER.

Royal College of Nursing (1994) *Violence and community nursing staff*, London: Royal College of Nursing.

Roys, P. (1988) 'Social services', in A. Bhat, R. Carr-Hill and S. Sushel, (eds) *Britain's Black population: A new perspective*, Aldershot: Gower.

SACHR (Standing Advisory Committee on Human Rights) (1987) *Religious and political discrimination and equality of opportunity in Northern Ireland report on fair employment*, Cmd 237, HMSO.

Schein, V., Mueller, R., Lituchy, T. and Liu, J. (1996) 'Think manager – think male: a global phenomenon', *Journal of Organisational Behaviour*, vol 17, no 1, pp 33-41.

Seccombe, I. and Smith, G. (1997) *Taking part: Registered nurses and the labour market*, London: Royal College of Nursing and Institute for Employment Studies.

Seccombe, I., Ball, J. and Patch, A. (1993) *The price of commitment: Nurses pay, careers and prospects*, Brighton: Institute of Manpower Studies.

Secretary of State (1998) *Modernising social services*, Cm 4169, London: The Stationery Office.

Seebohm Report (1968) *Report of the committee on local authority and allied personal social services*, London: HMSO.

Siefert, K., Jayaratne, S. and Chess, W. (1991) 'Job satisfaction, burnout and turnover in health care social workers', *Health and Social Work*, vol 16, no 3, pp 193-202.

Sinclair, I. and Gibbs, I. (1996) *Quality of care in children's homes: Working Paper Series B, no 3*, York: Social Work Research and Development Unit, University of York.

Skinner, A. (1992) *Another kind of home: A review of residential child care*, Edinburgh: HMSO.

SLGIU (Scottish Local Government Information Unit) (1998) *Guide to social work services in Scotland*, Glasgow: SLGIU.

Smale, G. (1996) *Managing change through innovation: Towards a model for developing and reforming social work practice and social service delivery*, London: NISW.

Smyth, M. (1996) *Qualified social workers and probation officers*, Office of National Statistics, London: HMSO.

Smyth, M. and Campbell, J. (1996) 'Social work, sectarianism and anti-sectarian practice in Northern Ireland', *British Journal of Social Work*, vol 26, no 1, pp 77-92.

SSI (Social Services Inspectorate) (1991) *Women in social services:A neglected resource*, London: HMSO.

SSI (1997) *Training support programme:A report on targets and achievements in 1995/6*, Report no 24, London: DoH.

Surrey County Council (1987) *Safe and secure in Surrey*, Surrey Social Services Department.

Taylor, C. (1994) 'Is gender inequality in social work management relevant to social work students?', *British Journal of Social Work*, vol 24, no 2, pp 157-72.

Thompson, N., Stradling, S., Murphy, M. and Neill, P.O. (1996) 'Stress and organisational culture', *British Journal of Social Work*, vol 26, no 5, pp 647-66.

Tisdall, E.K.M. (1997) *The Children (Scotland) Act, 1995: Developing policy and law for Scotland's children*, Edinburgh: Children in Scotland and The Stationery Office.

Tobin, J. and Carson, J. (1994) 'Stress and the student social worker', *Social Work and Social Sciences Review*, vol 5, no 3, pp 246-55.

TUC (Trade Union Congress) (1996) *The working time directive*, London: TUC.

Turner, M. (1997) *Shaping our lives:An interim report*, unpublished report available from the Policy Unit, NISW.

Utting, W. (1991) *Children in the public care:A review of residential care*, London: HMSO.

Virdee, S. (1995) *Racial violence and harassment*, London: PSI.

Wacjman, J. (1996) 'Desperately seeking differences: is management style gendered?', *British Journal of Industrial Relations*, vol 34, no 3, pp 333-49.

Wagner, G. (1988) *Residential care: A positive choice*, London: HMSO.

Warner, N. (1992) *Choosing with care: The report of the Committee of Inquiry into the selection, development and management of staff in children's homes*, London: HMSO.

Warr, P., Cook, J. and Wall, T. (1979) 'Scales for the measurement of some work attitudes and aspects of psychological well-being', *Journal of Occupational Psychology*, vol 52, pp 129-48.

Warr, P.B. (1987) *Work, unemployment and mental health*, Oxford: Clarendon Press.

Warren, L. (1990) '"We're home helps because we care": the experience of home helps caring for elderly people', in P. Abbott and G. Payne (eds) *New directions in the sociology of health*, London: Falmer Press, pp 70-86.

Webb, A. and Wistow, G. (1987) *Social care, social work and social planning: The personal social services*, Harlow: Longman.

Younghusband, E. (1978) *Social work in Britain: 1950 to 1975. A follow up study*, London: George Allen and Unwin.

Index

Please note: tables/figures are indicated by italics, unless there is related text on the same page.

educational 135, 150
need to enhance 191
professional 32–3, 141–2, 149–50,
  151–3
  and seniority 135, 138–9

R

racism 118–19, 186–7, 189, 191
  by employers 115, 116, 127
  by service users/relatives 117–18,
    126, 127
  and stress/support 119–20, *121,*
    127, 186
  in studies: method 108, 109
Registered Disabled Persons Act
  (1948) 79
relatives: of service users
  and racism 117–18, 126
  and violence 94, 95, 97, 105
reorganisation: of services/local
  government
  in England 182, 190–1
  and job changes/leaving 166, 167,
    173–4, 178, 185
  in Northern Ireland 13–14, 51,
    53, 58–9
  in Scotland 11, 51, 53, 58
Residential Child Care Initiative 142
residential homes: managers 39, 95
Residential Homes Act (1984) 6
residential staff
  and ethnicity/identity *113,* 114
  hours of work 44, *45*
  and job satisfaction 64–5, 76, 189
  pay 46, *47*
  research 4–5
  responsibilities 43, 57–9, 62
  seniority: factors 134, 138–9
  and stress 69–70, *72, 74, 82,* 171,
    179
  in studies: samples *18, 19, 20*
  training/qualifications 138–9, 145,
    150, 152–3, 157
    interest in 147, *148,* 174
    low level 4, 144, *149*
    via short courses 153, *154*

and violence 4–5, 92, *93,* 95–6,
  100, 104–5
  in Scotland 91, 92, *93, 100*
  stress/support *101, 102,* 179
work history 24, 26, 27, 39, 41
  career breaks 35, *136*
  job changes 30, 31, 166, 178,
    179, 183
  reasons for leaving 168–9, 173
  years employed 28, 29
Ross, E. 69

S

satisfaction, job 61, 62–7, 83, 172–3,
  179, 183
  and social care changes 60, 170–1,
    172, 185–6
  and stress/control 65, 75, 77–8,
    83–4, 184, 189–90
  and community identity 123, *124*
  and leaving work 168, 169–72
Scotland
  ethnic minorities 109
  social services 9–11
    in study: sample 12–13, *17,* 18,
      19, 20
  training: funding 142–3
Scottish Office 10–11, 142, 143
Scottish Vocational Qualifications
  (SVQs) 142, 152, 153, 159, 187
Seccombe, I. 131
sectarianism 109 *see also* community
  identity
Seebohm Report (1968) 5
self-study 154–5
seniority: attainment 133–9
  and gender 130–3, 138, 139–40
service users 43–4
  and discrimination 117–18, 122,
    126, 127
  and staff training 143, 147
  and stress *74,* 170–1, 184
  and violence 96–7
Sex Discrimination Act (1975) 183
short course training 153–4
sick leave: and stress 79–81